Writing Your Way Through College

Writing Your Way Through College
A Student's Guide

Sheryl I. Fontaine and Cherryl Smith

HEINEMANN
Portsmouth, NH

Heinemann

361 Hanover Street
Portsmouth, NH 03801–3912
www.heinemann.com

Offices and agents throughout the world

Library of Congress Cataloging-in-Publication Data
Fontaine, Sheryl I. and Smith, Cherryl.
    Writing your way through college : a student's guide / Sheryl I. Fontaine and Cherryl Smith.
        p. cm.
    Includes bibliographical references.
    ISBN-13: 978-0-86709-591-3
    ISBN-10: 0-86709-591-1
    1. English language—Rhetoric—Study and teaching (Higher). 2. Academic writing—Study and teaching (Higher). I. Title.
    PE1404.F66 2008
    808'.0420711—dc22   2007039069

Editor: Charles I. Schuster
Production editor: Sonja S. Chapman
Cover design: Night & Day Design
Cover photograph: Copyright © Getty Images, Inc.
Compositor: Kim Arney
Manufacturing: Louise Richardson

Printed in the United States of America on acid-free paper
17   16   15   14   13   VP   3   4   5   6   7

*This book is dedicated to our sons
David Fontaine-Boyd and Jeremy Smith-Danford,
for their laughter, patience, and wisdom.*

Contents

Acknowledgments

This textbook could not have been written without the participation of the students in our own writing classes. Though we were limited in the actual number of student essays we could include in this book, the spirit of many other students is woven through its pages. Beyond engaging in our classes for their own benefit, our students helped us to see the emerging text through their eyes, allowing us to hear the instructions and read the assignments as they do and then to write and revise from their perspective. We are grateful for their honesty. We are also grateful for the enthusiastic, collegial support of the tutors in the writing centers at California State University, Fullerton and California State University, Sacramento.

Our textual vision, once drafted, could not have become a reality without the expert staff at Heinemann who carefully listened to and read our ideas, shaping them into a form that could be shared with students and teachers. We especially want to thank Lisa Leudeke for her faith in and excitement about our work and our editor, Chuck Schuster, whose expertise, good humor, and encouragement provided sustenance as the book was being brought to life. During those years, we also relied on many friends whose emotional and intellectual support was both intentional on their parts and, more often, emerged unbidden from their kind and generous hearts.

Chapters in Order
of Writing Assignments

Writing Your Way Through College

CHAPTER
1

Getting Ready to Write

Reading and Writing for Essays 1 and 2

What Do You Expect to Find in This Book?

As you open this book, it would be interesting to think about what expectations you are bringing to it about college writing. Your individual expectations may be based on previous experiences you have had with writing textbooks or with writing in school, and some of your expectations may have emerged from ways you have seen college depicted on TV or in films, from conversations you have had with friends or relatives who have taken college writing courses, or from your own experiences in other college courses you have already completed. Your expectations for college writing may also be influenced by popular myths about what it means to write, particularly about what it means to write in college.

As composition professors, we are familiar with at least three beliefs about college writing that we would call myths. One myth is that writing is primarily the skill of learning certain rules and patterns that could have been mastered before entering college. We call this a myth because, as you will learn in this text, all writing occurs in a specific context, and these shifting contexts make it impossible for the art of writing ever truly to be mastered or for writers ever to finish growing and learning. Although you may have taken other courses that included writing assignments similar to those found at the university, they were, nevertheless, very context specific. Courses you took in high school, for example, may have increased your range of experience with writing and helped you gain confidence as a writer, but these courses in no way replace or make unnecessary a college writing class. This is because the constraints on a college writer—the expectations of the audience, the length of the assignments, and the writer's relationship to his or her subject matter—are different from those that occur in any other context. College writing is the form of written communication found in the academic world of universities and colleges—and nowhere else.

A second common myth is that writing courses are not really about anything, that they lack subject matter and are simply prerequisites for the "real" writing students do in their other college classes. We argue in this book, however, that there is nothing preliminary about college writing courses. First, there is subject matter related to the study of writing. The academic discipline of Composition and Rhetoric is devoted to the study of writing, to researching and theorizing about every aspect of what it means to write. This study informs what is taught in college writing classes. Second, any time you write, you must choose some subject to learn about or reflect on with enough sustained attention that you find thoughts of your own to express. This book and the writing course you are currently taking do not present you with the prerequisites for writing at college but provide you with the experience of *being* a college writer.

A final myth about college writing is that it is something you can take in a semester or two and get over with quickly. The writing placement exams and discretely defined writing requirements at many colleges falsely suggest that writing can be mastered once and for all before you enter college or by the end of a specific course or two. You may have the impression that one need only learn a particular format or some new vocabulary in order for the difficulties of college writing to be resolved.

However, it is important to remember that all writing requires creativity and involves writers in a process of using language to create new meanings in new contexts. Whether you are enrolled in basic or advanced writing, freshman composition or a senior seminar, or you are writing on your own, every phrase, every sentence you write, has never been said just that way before, nor has it appeared before in precisely that context. Presented with this endless variety of contexts in which to write, no writer—college or professional—can ever really finish learning how to write.

 Reflection
Your Expectations, Fears, and Hopes About Writing

After taking a few minutes to reflect on the following questions, write out your thoughts for each one: Do the myths about college writing classes that we have described sound familiar? What other beliefs or myths have you brought with you? What do you expect will change for you as a writer by the time you finish this course? What fears do you have about college writing? What do you imagine might get in the way of your development as a writer? What do you hope to learn?

Using This Book

This text is a resource for understanding the setting of college writing; it is something like a tour book that is helpful when you are traveling or have moved to a new city. It is a book to help you find your way, to help you understand the unusual signs and odd markings on the map. This book can also help you see yourself in relation to this particular territory in which you are traveling. There are certain customs to college writing that may seem unusual in relation to your previous experiences; places of particular interest to be visited; blind alleys that might be avoided or, at least, identified; there are names that may require translation.

Although writing at college certainly resembles writing outside of college, the academic environment where it takes place is, in a sense, a community with its own set of expectations and values. The positions of authority that academics are expected to hold and the kind of value that academics place on conveying knowledge result in language and essay structures that may be, to the outsider, mysterious or imposing. This book provides an insider's view. You will find information about kinds of writing courses and assignments, about how teachers and programs evaluate writing, about the demands of college writing and ways to meet those demands, and about the particular expectations of the various disciplines and majors that make up the college curriculum.

Our aim, in *Writing Your Way Through College*, is to familiarize you with the idiosyncrasies of the college writing community and with the particular ways of using language that you will encounter in college. At the same time, we want to help you use the language experiences you already have to make college writing personally meaningful and, ultimately, to provide your writing with a sense of purpose and focus. What we have learned through many years of teaching college writing and through our own experiences as academic writers is that writing well, at the university or elsewhere, depends on not only understanding the expectations of one's audience but finding one's own identity as a writer. The voice in which you write and the language you use to shape ideas grow from your own individual experiences, from your cultural background and history, and from your sense of yourself both as a writer and as an individual. While introducing you to the culture of the academic environment as it relates to writing, our goal is also to help you identify personal and cultural resources that bring you power as a writer and that can be your foundation for writing in college.

Beyond helping you develop the connection between yourself and the ideas about which you are writing, our final aim for *Writing Your Way Through College* is to remind you that as a college writer, you are not alone. Although writers usually compose by themselves, writing is very much a social activity; to some degree, all writing is part of a collaboration with a number of individuals who, themselves, bring to the writing situation their own set of experiences and cultural histories. College writing puts you into an interaction with instructors, other students, professional writers, and scholars, with people who may be sitting right next to you and with others whom you will never, could never, meet.

As a student, sometimes you may choose to sit quietly at the back of a classroom, listening to and recording material from a lecture. Other times you may sit silently at your desk, reading and recording information from a written text. In both cases, as a listener and as a reader, you have the option to be still, even to remain detached, as you hear or read someone else's words. When you write, however, it is impossible to remain detached. Intentionally or not, your own words and identity create a connection between yourself and the material about which you are writing. Furthermore, your words create a connection between yourself and your reader.

---

2 Reflection
Sharing Expectations, Fears, and Hopes About Writing

Read aloud or exchange your Reflection 1 with another member of the class. When you are listening or reading, your job is to take in what the writer has to say—his or her expectations, fears, and hopes about writing—to listen or read attentively and nonjudgmentally. Give yourself a chance to reread the writing or to hear it again one or more times.

Write your reactions to what your classmate said. How is his or her experience different from or similar to your own? Offer your own insights into what he or she has said. You might raise questions, if you have some, and write about what the other's reflection triggers in your own thinking.

Writing to Find Meaning

One overarching conclusion we make from our own academic writing experience and our work with college writers is that the single best way to improve your writing is to immerse yourself in writing, to write as much and as reflectively as you can. If you write a note like this: "Gone to the gym—be back around 7:00," you are using writing to record and convey information. To produce this kind of writing, you usually compose quickly and without much thought since you already know what you want to say. Of course, most of the writing you do in college involves not merely recording something you already know, but using written language to help figure out what you want to say—even to help figure out what you do not yet know. When we write reflectively, in thoughtful and examining ways, we do much more than record our thoughts for later reference. If we give ourselves the opportunity to write freely and deeply, without limiting ourselves, writing actually can help us to understand our own thoughts, experiences, and observations in a way we would not have otherwise.

We arrived at this conclusion, that writing is a tool for understanding and reflecting, after many years of research and study. Donald Murray (2004), Anne Lamott (1995), Anne Berthoff (1981), and Janet Emig (1983) all demonstrate from their experiences as teachers, writers, and researchers that writing can lead us to make connections that would not be visible to us otherwise. And although it is certainly not necessary for you to have read this research in order to write well, throughout the text, we will identify authors whose works we recommend if you are interested in learning more about writing.

When any of us write, the words we put on a sheet of paper or computer screen have emerged from a long journey, most of which has taken place without our awareness. Before we write—or even speak—we experience a sense of wanting to say something, a physical or emotional desire to express a thought. Drawing on the work of Eugene Gendlin (1982), writer and theorist Sondra Perl (2004) explains that we have a "felt sense" of our thoughts even before we may be able to articulate them in words.

Finding words for our felt sense is a natural process that often happens so quickly we are unaware of it. In everyday speaking, this process usually takes place quite rapidly, and as we attempt to express ourselves, our minds select and reject several possible words or phrases instantaneously. However, since we cannot write as quickly as we can speak, when we write, this process occurs more slowly, and so we may notice ourselves shuttling back and forth between our sense of what we want to say and the words we are finding. As the match between our sense of what we want to say and the words we choose becomes closer, we may become more conscious of our choices. Although much of the time, in both speaking and writing, we find the words we're seeking, sometimes we may labor in our search. In speaking, if we are trying to figure something out or grapple with a difficult idea, we may struggle a bit with our words or interrupt ourselves to say more clearly what we are thinking. Sometimes we pause, rephrase an idea, or reject our statement altogether. When we write, these pauses can bog down our progress as we struggle to find words that capture what we are feeling and thinking. It is then that writers are likely to complain, "I know what I want to say. I just can't write it!"

Yet something powerful is happening during this struggle. As we reject words, selecting only those that come closest to our sense of what we are trying to say, we are taking something that is vague and intangible and crystallizing it into visible, written language. This is a complicated process. We make connections between our initial felt sense and the words we use; we create new thoughts that would not have existed had we not attempted to represent our ideas and feelings in words. When we find just the right word or phrase, when we reach an "I got it!" moment, we are experiencing the power of language to help us find meaning. We discover we can learn from our own writing.

Exploratory Writing

To help themselves focus on the emerging meaning of their writing, many writers make use of freewriting, a technique that you may already know and that we ourselves learned from Peter Elbow (1980), Ken Macrorie (1985), and other teachers. This technique is also sometimes called quickwriting, nonstop writing, brainstorming, and exploratory writing. Because it is the most useful strategy we know for generating writing, we have incorporated freewriting extensively into the writing tasks assigned in *Writing Your Way Through College*.

One of the difficulties of writing is that since it is slower than speaking, we have more time to get in our own way. That is, we may tend to criticize our work even before figuring out what we are going to say. In the process of shuttling back and forth between our felt sense and the written words, we may pause so long to debate our choice of words that we lose our train of thought. Or we might think ahead to how a reader may view our writing, worrying whether we have said something correctly to such an extent that we can't concentrate on the meaning. Mike Rose (1985), has described the difficulty that writers can experience when these "rigid rules" block their ability to write freely. Freewriting takes advantage of the meaning-making power of written language by removing these blocks that can keep us from letting words guide our writing; it focuses our attention on whatever felt sense is emerging as we write.

When you freewrite, you are able to shut out the critic in your head who distracts you from thinking about what you are writing with worries about how you are writing. Instead of pushing ahead, following the ideas you are generating, the critic nags at you to pause and rewrite, edit, cross out, get a cup of coffee, send a text message—anything that will prevent you from attentively and insistently writing to capture what it is you want to say. In order to use freewriting to silence that critic, you must do two things: *write without stopping* and *write without rereading or correcting*. Just keep your pen or cursor moving, even if you write, "I'm stuck, I'm stuck, I'm stuck," or "What'll I say? What'll I say?" until you find you've moved on to saying something else. There will be time later for rereading, revising, editing, or discarding what you've written; while you are freewriting just keep the flow of thought pouring onto the page or computer screen.

Freewriting is a way of brainstorming or free-associating. At first, it may seem like a difficult (or counterproductive) task to write without worrying about writing well. But with practice it becomes easier and, as many professional writers, teachers, and researchers have attested (see Belanoff, Elbow, and Fontaine 1991) and as you yourself will see, because it helps you to generate writing, to get your ideas down, freewriting is a powerful technique for developing your abilities as a writer.

Freewriting About an Idea

Most of the time, writers do not compose an entirely free-associative kind of freewriting. Freewriting, in which you write anything at all that is on your mind, is the way you are likely to write in a private journal or a letter, or an email to someone you know well or, occasionally, to a wider, less familiar audience. It is the best way to get feelings, first impressions, or initial thoughts down in words on screen or paper. However, even in entirely free-associative freewriting, our natural tendency is to focus on particular subjects or ideas, to follow the lines of our thinking in particular directions.

Just as you can use freewriting to explore and create ideas, you can also use it to focus on any specific ideas you find interesting. Often, writers begin their freewriting in this way, with the intention of focusing on a particular subject, what Peter Elbow (1998) calls "focused freewriting." Rather than write randomly what comes to mind, you write what comes to mind on a certain question or subject you wish to analyze. The idea you begin with provides both a starting place and a reference point as you compose—nonstop—without your critic's nagging interference. Freewriting can help you explore an idea, expand your sense of what that idea is, refine your understanding of it, or see connections between this idea and others.

---

3   **Reflection**
Trying Out and Reflecting on Freewriting

1. Freewrite for six or seven minutes about any topic or idea that comes to mind. You do not have to write quickly, just steadily, without pausing to reread or make changes as you write.

2. Starting with the topic of "what keeps me from writing," freewrite for another six or seven minutes, letting your thoughts and writing travel wherever they want within that general topic.

3. Reread what you wrote for steps 1 and 2 and write for a few minutes about the experiences of freewriting. What surprised you or frustrated you? How did having a topic as a starting point seem to affect the writing? Are there differences in structure or style between the two pieces of writing? Did you write things that you would not have predicted?

Reading and Writing in This Text

Writing Your Way Through College uses both reading and writing to engage you in the kind of specialized, insider conversation shared by people who work in the same place or study the same subject. This textbook asks you to read about college writing as it is perceived by people who study the subject closely and then to write your own college essays in six different assignments.

In the first part of *Writing Your Way Through College*, we have included information about the way one speaks and writes within various language communities; about the history of college writing and your place in this history; and about how one learns the conventions of language communities, especially the communities of academic disciplines. Following this introduction, Chapters 2 and 3 describe the ways in which people find themselves moving through many language communities in the course of a single day or over the course of a lifetime. An awareness of how we shift language communities in daily life is useful as you move through the college writing community. Chapters 4 and 5 focus on the particular language community of college, the one in which you currently find yourself. These chapters talk about the historical evolution of college writing in the academic community and provide ways for you to think about how you, as an individual, intersect with that history today. Because each area or discipline has its own unique set of conventions and expectations, Chapters 6 and 7 move from the general college language community to the specific one of your major area of study. These chapters examine how we come to see and know the conventions of academic language communities and, ultimately, how you, as a student, can identify and use them in your prospective major.

Interspersed with reading about these topics, we ask you to reflect, in quick, focused freewriting, on what you have read. The reflections, like the ones you already completed earlier in this chapter, ask you to pause in your reading and to use freewriting as a way of thinking about what you have read, making connections between and among ideas, and making meaning of all of this for yourself. The reflections represent your first thoughts or impressions about what you have read, so they may vary in length and depth. Some questions we provide and some sections of the text will rouse more reaction and response from you than others. As a general guideline, spend at least ten minutes freewriting; sometimes this will be all the time that is needed and other times you will want to go on longer. You can think of the reflections as ideas in the making—first impressions, thoughts, and reactions.

At the same time that the reflections will serve as a way to record and examine your thoughts, they will also provide you with ideas that can be used in the essay assignments that appear in Part 2 of the text. As you read each chapter and complete its corresponding reflections, you will be creating material that may serve as starting points for your essays. Consequently, the more thought you devote to the reflections, the more ready you will be for drafting an essay when you get to that point in the process.

All of the essay assignments included in Part 2 of *Writing Your Way Through College* are instances of college writing, that is, writing that uses a particular source of information in order to analyze a subject and find evidence for the purpose of conveying an explicitly stated focus or meaning. With the goal of identifying and, ultimately, conveying an explicit focus or meaning, you will be asked to select a subject to write about and a source of information from which to analyze and produce appropriate evidence.

In this text, we identify three sources of evidence that inform all college writing: evidence that emerges from conversation and observation, from the writer's own recollections and memories, and from written texts. Each essay you write will reflect on and analyze a specific subject using one or more of these sources to identify a focus and the points of evidence you will use to support and develop that idea. Essay assignments 1, 3, and 5 ask you to address subjects or questions about language and writing that have emerged from reading Part 1 of *Writing Your Way Through College*. Essays 2, 4, and 6 ask you to write about subjects or questions that interest you personally about any topic you choose.

Each assignment includes exploratory writing activities designed to help you discover ideas and find the focus of your essay. These activities will help you to analyze your material from multiple perspectives in order to identify what you want to write about, to reflect on the subject, to focus your writing, and to determine what additional evidence you need to support your points.

Part 3 of the text includes three chapters that are intended to help you as you draft and revise your essays. First, we have provided several pieces of writing that our own students have completed while using this text. Rather than thinking about these as models or best examples, consider these essays as providing you and your classmates with the opportunity to examine and discuss how other student writers handled the same writing assignments you will be facing. In each essay, we have embedded questions that will help you to think about different ways that writers focus their writing and use their gathered information to make and support their ideas.

The last two chapters in the book, "Guidelines for Reading and Responding to Writers' Drafts" and "Guidelines for Editing Final Revisions," can be used as you move from a rough draft of your essay to a more focused and well-supported revision and, finally, to a clean, well-edited final copy. First we provide instructions and questions for classmates or friends to answer about your draft so that you can learn how well you are conveying and supporting the focus of your essay. The last chapter provides a similar list of questions that you can use in order to edit the grammar, syntax, and spelling in your nearly completed essays.

CHAPTER
2

Situating Ourselves in Language

Reading and Writing for Essays 1 and 2

Integrating Your Own Voice with Others' Voices

We begin with an assertion: Your language, what you say and the way you say it, represents much more than just you, an individual person. Although all of us necessarily draw on our own personal experiences, feelings, values, and understandings, we do not do this in isolation. Rather, our voices, the stories we choose to tell, the words we select, and the way we put words together, emerge from thousands of competing and contributing voices that surround us. Each day, we find ourselves in numerous situations where other people's words shape our views of reality and the way we use language.

Examples of this interplay of language are easy to identify. Here are two that might occur at a movie theater. First, imagine that while waiting in line outside the theatre you overhear a woman in the next line talking about the film you are about to see. "The acting was really bad," you hear her say. "Half the time, I couldn't even follow the story. Oh, and the ending—it's really unbelievable." Even if you are determined to tune out her opinion and have your own, you cannot unhear what she has said. In some way her review may stay with you as you watch the film and form your own judgments. To some degree, judgments you make about the film may be a response to her words.

Now imagine that during the film, a central character or several characters repeat a particular phrase such as "Go ahead, make my day" or "My precious" or "May the Force be with you." Though your attention was initially on the scene in which the actors uttered the phrase, you may leave the theatre taking the phrase with you and find yourself using it in your own, everyday life, a life that probably differs greatly from that of the movie characters.

These two scenarios suggest that even though we do have our own, unique thoughts and we select our own words, our words and thoughts also emerge from a whirlwind of language of which we are all a part. In the example of waiting in the movie line, your thinking about the film, even the way you perceive it, may be influenced by the language you encountered as you waited in line. In the second example of hearing memorable phrases in a movie, words from one context—in this case, the way words were used in a film—become adapted to the contexts of your own life. As you develop as a writer, you are likely to find yourself growing more conscious of the interconnectedness of language use, and we encourage you to pause and listen to some of these voices around you, to the ways in which your individual perspective is influenced by and, in turn, influences others' thoughts and words.

 Reflection
Telling the Same Story from Another Perspective

Think of a recent conversation, argument, or experience you had. Write down the details of what happened. Who said what? What were points of disagreement and agreement? What do you remember most about the experience?

Now, write the details from the perspective of someone else who was involved in this same conversation or argument or experience. If possible, ask someone who was there to tell you about the experience, and take notes on that person's recollection. Reread your notes and compare them with what you first wrote. Or write what you believe the conversation might have looked like from the other person's perspective. Finally, write about the similarities and differences you see in the two versions of the story.

Defining Language Communities

As a writer, you choose words and create a voice belonging to you and representing your individuality. Yet your words also exist separately from you as a part of a vast, verbal network of language—the stories, exclamations, commands, questions, statements, and so on within which we all live. As this profusion of words and language circles around us, we take some of it in, and it influences the way we name and perceive the world. At the same time, none of us is merely an observer and absorber of language; we are all participants who adapt and filter language through our own experiences and thought processes. To varying degrees, our interaction with language has an effect on those around us, on others' thinking, and on the words they use.

But this network of language is complex. It is not as if there were a single, generic English language for all situations. Instead, we encounter many language situations, each with differing characteristics and conventions. While the same words may be used, they take on different emphases or meanings depending on the context. What is appropriate in one set of circumstances might be wildly inappropriate in another. You are likely to greet close friends differently than you greet your elderly relatives; the way you address your professor is likely to be different from the way you address young children in your family; the conversations you might overhear at a football game are likely to be different from those overheard at a religious service. Imagine walking into the operating room of a hospital while a team of doctors and nurses is undertaking a complicated surgical procedure. The language around you would be quite distinct from, for instance, the language you might hear if you walked into a session of the state legislature or into a café in the student union. Each of these circumstances is made distinct by the variables comprising the language situation: the specialized vocabulary they include, the tone the speakers use, and the purposes for which people are speaking.

In the related fields of psycholinguistics and linguistics, Martin Nystrand (1982) and John Swales (1990), having observed the way people use language, concluded that when language situations are distinct and well defined from each other in terms of their characteristics and conventions, they can be identified as specific *communities*. Because the members of any community understand a common set of terminology and expectations for what is talked about and in what manner, they share a common way of using language. However, even though they have unique, and often difficult-to-understand, features that are well known to *only their own* members, language communities are fluid and overlap with each other so that outside or new members can understand much that is said.

Beneath the surface of any language situation is a complex interplay of psychological, social, and linguistic features that affect, almost automatically, how speakers interact. In each circumstance, as a speaker, you will feel varying degrees of comfort or unfamiliarity, informality or distance. Speakers can give conscious attention to how they want to fit themselves into a particular language situation, and in this way they can effectively *situate* themselves in the language being used. That is, they can speak in ways that are comfortable for themselves and believable to listeners. Consider this contrast: Were you to join the conversation in an operating room, you would likely be tongue-tied and unsure about where to jump in, both because you are unfamiliar with the language and because a misuse of language might result in a life-threatening error. But among friends in a local coffee shop, you are likely to feel relatively at ease adding to the conversation. Because you are familiar with the words, their particular uses, and the topics most frequently discussed, you can add to the conversation at the expected moments in the expected, appropriate ways.

---

5 Reflection
An Unfamiliar or Difficult Language Situation

Make a list of moments, from school or personal experiences, in which you found yourself in an unfamiliar or difficult language situation. Choose one of the moments, perhaps the one you recall most vividly. Share your experiences with a classmate by telling the stories in class or emailing them to each other. When you do so, include what you remember about the places, participants, emotions, and events. After hearing or reading one another's stories, ask questions if there is further information that seems to be needed.

Write your reflections on your or your classmate's stories. What characteristics did your shared moments have in common? What are some of the qualities of these difficult or unfamiliar language experiences?

Establishing the Authority to Be Heard

The familiarity or confusion you feel in a language situation also affects the authority with which you speak, authority that allows you to situate yourself successfully in the conversation. For you to gain this authority, there also must be a parallel shift in the perception of people with whom you are speaking. That is, rather than see you as an outsider, disconnected from the conversation, others must perceive you as a member of the conversation and, consequently, give you the opportunity to speak and to be heard.

In most situations, these shifts of perception are subtle. While in some settings you might be formally called upon to speak, in most situations you merely sense you are a member of the conversation by others' gestures, word choice, and mode of response, and by whether someone looks in your direction, makes eye contact, or leans toward you slightly, nodding to draw out your comments.

As a speaker, you have some influence on the extent to which others see you as having authority, as having the right to contribute to an ongoing conversation and be heard. To enter into a conversation and be comfortably situated in its language, you find a position from which to speak that is both authentic and valuable to you and that, at the same time, will hold the attention of those listening. Without authenticity or personal connection, your speech would neither interest nor be convincing to a listener.

For example, if you tried to participate in the operating room conversation as if you were a full-fledged member of the surgical team, or if you stood up in the state legislature posing as a senator, you might even be asked to leave. But if you spoke to the surgeons from a position you really held, that of someone who had a particular interest in the surgery under way because the patient was a relative, or if in the state legislature you provided, from your perspective as a student, a commentary on the bill under discussion, which would have an impact on the availability of student loans, you would be establishing your authority because you would be speaking authentically from an authoritative position you actually held.

In many situations—sitting in the student union, for instance—you do not need to give conscious attention to gaining the authority to speak; since you have the same status as others involved in the conversation, your speaking privilege is much easier to establish. Yet any language situation may be uncomfortable at first. Even the most confident among us may feel initially ill at ease the first time she enters the student union and would most certainly feel awkward engaging in conversation with surgeons in the fictional operating room we have mentioned. No matter how sure you are of yourself and what you want to say, it takes remaining in a particular setting for a while, listening to the conversation, and trying out your own responses to overcome any initial feelings of being out of place.

As a student, you have entered the language community of college writing and must examine what perspectives you can offer to give authority to your voice and your words. As in any language community, at your college or university you will learn to situate yourself appropriately and authentically in relation to the conventions and expectations of the community so that your words will be convincing to a listener or reader.

---

6 Reflection
Speaking as an Authority

In this reflection, we ask you to speak from a position of authority you already hold. First, jot down subjects about which *you* have some expertise. You may be an expert on certain academic subjects, sports, hobbies; you may know about certain cities, countries, languages; you may have specific life experiences or interests about which you know a great deal. After you have compiled your list, choose one subject to tell about, or ask the classmate you are partnering with to help you choose one. Next, tell your classmate about your subject while he takes notes, and then make notes as your class-mate speaks on his or her subject. Find out as much as you can about each other's sub-jects. When you have both spoken, reread your notes.

After reading your notes, write about what you learned or noticed, from listening to your classmate or from telling him about your subject, about what happens when we speak as an authority.

Language Situations Close to Home

As we have suggested, you have been negotiating among various language commu-nities all your life without necessarily giving conscious attention to it. Your expertise at navigating these situations is evident if you consider the language you speak and hear in the communities with which you are most familiar, those in your home or among your close friends. When we communicate with people who are closest to us, there are times when we are concerned about how to approach a particular subject, times when we debate inside ourselves about when would be the best moment to ask a specific question, times when we feel unable to say what we want to say. However, even on these occasions, when we find ourselves searching for the best approach to take, our choices are part of a well-established pattern that is familiar.

Among these familiar communities, the most recognizable are those that occur in one's family. Here, your right to speak, to engage in conversation, to make state-ments, ask questions, and so on, and the authority with which you do so are closely tied to your role in the family and the relationships you have with other family mem-bers. Part of this role is defined by your position in the family as a son, daughter, mother, father, husband, wife, partner, brother, sister, cousin, or any other such role or position that remains constant and affects, in predictable ways, how people in the family converse. For example, a parent might be expected to be the dominant mem-ber of a conversation with a child; an elder sibling might have more authority than the younger.

At the same time, although you continue in your role, circumstances change as you grow older or new members come into the family, to some degree shifting the conversational structure. The effects of family history, ethnic and religious tra-ditions, regional style, and economic influences help define particular family and speaking positions. Roles for women, children, eldest siblings, parents of the hus-band, and other specific positions may affect what the authority structure will be. The degree of responsibility, respect, and authority that your role holds was estab-lished with your entrance into, or the formation of, your family, and it evolves as you age and mature and as your family evolves.

Have a conversation or exchange emails with a classmate about how authority seems to be established and demonstrated in language situations in your respective families. Describe to each other some typical conversations that might occur among family members. Who are the dominant speakers? What are some distinctive language patterns in the family? How do different members of the family establish or relinquish authority?

Write some observations about what qualities determine authority in language situations that occur in your and your classmate's families.

Coded Language

For children, the language we have been describing begins in their families. Once friendships begin to form outside of the family, children become part of other language communities that are close to, but outside of, the home. Similar to the language of families, the speaking patterns and relationships among close friends are shaped, in part, by the speakers' shared history and become well established over time. Furthermore, language conventions we use at home and with close friends and the relationships we establish with people close to us are grounded in a history that reaches back beyond our own, individual lives, to the way grandparents spoke to parents and great-grandparents spoke to them. This history extends beyond our own homes to the homes of past generations in our family and the families of our friends. Collectively, language history connects through these individuals to the cultures in which they lived. So while our close-to-home language is like that of other people of the same generation and culture, each home language is unique because it evolved from specific people in specific situations.

We can understand the conversation of people outside our own, close communication circle, but our understanding is to some degree limited by the fact that we have not shared the years of circumstances and events in which their conversation is embedded. Any language that is close to home includes a kind of code that consists of words or phrases that have particular meaning to the members of this family, to groups of friends, or to those who share a common history.

When members of a family speak different languages or dialects, sometimes with different levels of proficiency, a home language can become a unique combination of the original language of that family and the second or third languages that have been brought into the family more recently. To a certain extent, every family's language is such a combination, because different family members bring home with them particular dialects or slang from the communities they frequent outside the family. When a young teenager turns to his grandmother and says, "Awesome," in response to her question "How was the school party?" a cross-dialect code is being created, one whose success relies on each speaker understanding the other's ways of speaking, ways that might not be immediately or completely understood by a visitor to the family.

In fact, codedness is what distinguishes the language of communities close to home from that of the more distant language communities we discuss in Chapter 3. Some of the language used within families or groups of friends is particularly rich in metaphor and imagery; speakers refer to a whole sequence of shared experience in a few words, describing specific behavior or reflecting on a past event in a kind of shorthand. Over time, they may have created names for certain foods, games, moods, places, or events that are now part of an everyday vocabulary. This language is highly audience specific; you have to be part of the group to fully understand it.

---

8 **Reflection**
Identifying Code Language

First, list some of the phrases, words, names, or references you use in any of your close communication circles that you expect others outside that circle may not understand or, at least, might not understand in the same way you do. Once you have your list, exchange with someone in the class. Each of you should then write out what you imagine to be the definitions of the other's words and phrases. Then tell one another what the real definitions are and where they came from.

Write some observations about the nature of these code languages—where they seem to emerge from, how and when they are used, or what makes them effective codes whose meaning is restricted to family or group members.

Language Communities Farther from Home

If the language communities through which we all move weave a continuum of language use, at one end would be the most focused, audience-specific language communities such as those you were thinking about in the last reflection, and at the other end would be language that is available to the widest, most general audience. In between these two extremes are many language communities that are familiar to you. These communities may be demarcated by distinct, physical boundaries or by more abstract, intangible qualities. A language community may be defined by the streets or natural structures that frame a particular neighborhood or by a larger geographic area, such as a region or state. Or a language community may be formed less concretely, by cultural, ethnic, religious, socioeconomic, interest, or lifestyle identifications.

Although these language communities are much larger and more diverse than those of friends and families, like the smaller communities, they also share some degree of constancy. To some extent the language of a community helps distinguish and define it and, in the long term, helps keep it alive.

Reflection
Language Communities Connected to Your Classroom

Make a list of some of the language communities beyond your friends and family of which you are a part. Depending on your life experience, you might identify a neighborhood, geographic area, ethnic group, religious affiliation, or lifestyle as part of a distinctive community. Select one community from your list and, pairing with a classmate, interview each other about the particular languages of your respective communities. You might ask about some of the typical topics, specific speaking styles, or distinguishing features of language in your classmate's community. Or ask what stories your classmate can tell that illustrate some aspects of the language community. Make notes on what you are told and what you learn.

Once you are done, read through your notes and write about what you noticed or learned. How would you characterize the similarities and differences you see in the two communities and the languages and ways of speaking that they use?

Language Conventions in Careers and Interests

Before completing our discussion of familiar language communities, we would like to consider one additional type of community: that formed by individuals who share a specific interest or a career. One establishes one's membership in the kinds of language communities we have been describing by being born into, physically moving into, or making some other kind of deep commitment to a group. Those language communities do not depend upon outside learning or training to establish one's membership. One moves into a particular neighborhood, is born or adopted into a certain family, or is part of a particular ethnic group. Yet when groups of people share particular, learned interests, they also form a community and develop certain coded ways of communicating. These kinds of communities fall between the familiar language community groups we have been describing and the more general ones of wider communication that we discuss in the next chapter. Most jobs or intense hobbies require individuals to use at least some language that sounds unfamiliar to outsiders. This could be the engineering talk of a garage mechanic or an aerospace designer, the horticultural talk of a weekend gardener or landscape architect, the specialized talk of musicians and dedicated fans, or the conversations taking place on various websites and blogs dedicated to particular interests. The range of language communities available to us is seemingly unlimited.

 ### 10 Reflection
Identifying Language Conventions of Careers and Interests

Ask a friend or classmate to tell you about his or her career or avocation or area of interest. Make notes on what you learn about the way the friend speaks. Ask him or her to share with you some of the language of that community and the way in which it is most likely to be used. Write about what you learn.

CHAPTER
3

The Language of
Wider Communication

Reading and Writing for Essays 1 and 2

What Happens to Language when You Leave Familiar Surroundings?

The familiar language communities to which we are connected are, in some ways, defined by specific places: neighborhoods, homes, and so on. But familiar language communities are sustained over time, not so much by where they take place, but by the relationships and shared experiences among the individuals participating in them. For example, no matter where you meet your siblings or parents or spouse, you are likely to speak with them in certain predictable ways using familiar kinds of slang, phrases, and intonations. Change of location is not likely to change these qualities in your speech patterns. If you see a neighbor or someone you know from a close, community connection when you are traveling, you quickly fall into a familiar style of conversation. Odds are good that you will even talk about events in the neighborhood or your shared community group as much as, or more than, you will talk about the place you are visiting.

Language of Wider Communication

Naturally, each of us speaks daily with many people who are from neither our family nor our neighborhood, who don't belong to any of our close or familiar language communities. Often, in these situations, the most immediate concern is that communication is effective and efficient. When you find yourself at a stoplight needing directions and you roll down your window to ask the woman in the car next to you if she can help, you don't care or expect to hear where she went to high school or that she has twin brothers who play soccer. You want to know how to get to your destination, and you are hoping to get the information before the light changes. When you call the electric company because the power shut down as you were printing out an essay, you will be impatient if the person who answers your call speaks in unfamiliar phrases ("We are experiencing a temporary circuit breaker malfunction"). You just want to know how long it will be before you can finish printing your essay and if you can do so before class starts.

In these situations, and the hundreds of others like them, you use and expect to hear forms of spoken or written English that are general enough to allow individuals from an enormous number and variety of language communities to communicate intelligibly with one another. Geneva Smitherman (1977/1986; Smitherman-Donaldson 1987) was the first to call this form of English the "language of wider communication." What is most distinctive about this communication is that it attempts to sound *not* distinctive at all. It is the language most usually heard in the business world, at universities, and in public life in the United States. When people converse in situations requiring this kind of communication, most of the unique or distinguishing language features from familiar communities are set aside. Washed away from the language are qualities that could not be readily understood by a broad range of individuals, by people who do not know each other or share a common body of knowledge or similar personal histories.

Conventions of the Language of Wider Communication

The language of wider communication achieves its less personal, more efficient, and more direct quality in part through the use of standardized American English. Indeed, the language of wider communication is sometimes referred to as *Standard English* because it uses the standardized or most widely accepted conventions of English word usage, verb tense, pronoun reference, and agreement. Although code words used with family and other familiar communities work their way into this standardized form of communication, essentially, the farther we move from close communication communities, the fewer code words we use.

Whereas conventions of other language communities identify the speaker as a member of a particular social, ethnic, regional, or economic group, as a common language with standardized conventions, the language of wider communication may appear not to be attached to any particular language community. However, contrary to what the adjective *standard*, may suggest, the language of wider communication in the United States is, indeed, very much attached to a particular language community, but not the community of the original European settlers, nor that of the original inhabitants of America.

While English itself initially became the dominant language only because its community of speakers was larger than those of other languages coming into America, as the populations of immigrants shifted, other languages easily could have competed with English. As the shape of the newly colonized country progressed, the dominance of English became historically grounded in the social, political, and economic history of the country, a history that continues to the present time.

Standardized English conventions, rather than the conventions of other dialects of English, are used in the language of wider communication primarily because they have been adopted by the middle and upper classes in America. Because these speakers have had the greatest political impact on American life by virtue of their education and economic position, their ways of speaking became dominant (see Fox 1999). American dialects differ structurally, in the ways that verbs are formed, for example, but they don't differ in their capacity to allow speakers to express complex thought, discuss philosophy, conduct business, or convey emotion. Working-class dialects and dialects of any one ethnic minority group did not become the standardized dialect in America because they have not been connected positively to professional standing or economic power in this country. It is possible to write a scholarly paper, a business plan, or a powerful poem in any dialect. Yet rarely is there the opportunity to be heard widely unless one writes in the standardized dialect. Although this dialect actually represents a particular language community, the language of wider communication is considered the preferred dialect and has been claimed as the common language in which educated Americans are expected to be fluent.

 Reflection

Re-creating the Language of Wider Communication

Listen in (unobtrusively) on a conversation somewhere where you are likely to hear the language of wider communication—at the library, the financial aid office, in a bank, in the writing center—any place where communication seems to require that all speakers use what we have been calling the language of wider communication. Take notes on what you hear in as much detail as you can, listening especially for instances of standardized communication. Reread your notes and write briefly about the features of the language of wider communication you noticed and how they affected the conversation exchange that you overheard.

Code Switching: Related Risks and Biases

Speakers learn to code switch as they move from one language community to another. Code switching from familiar language communities to the language of wider communication can be illustrated by thinking of the way a clerk in a small store in an isolated town might speak while handling a transaction and the way the bank manager of a large city's main office might speak. The clerk knows most of the people who come into the store; she speaks the particular dialect of that community and has many shared experiences with her customers. The language she uses reflects this shared history; she addresses people by name or with some familiar greeting appropriate in that community. Were you a resident of the town, you would expect to visit with the clerk while you were completing your business, and the language of your visit would include code words—slang, particular references—that people from outside the community might not understand.

Think now of the city bank manager: Let's say she is the sister of the clerk we just described; she speaks fluently the language of the small town where she grew up, yet while conducting business in her capacity as bank manager of the large city's main office, she speaks in the language of wider communication. Here, visiting with customers would be not only inappropriate but nearly impossible given the lack of shared history of the people who frequent the bank. Essentially, the manager's speech must represent not only herself but the bank as well. The manager's language would sound more neutral and probably would be less interesting than her sister's. It would be language that anyone, from any part of the large city, could be expected to understand and would expect to hear.

Expecting to hear the language of wider communication in the bank's main branch, customers would be surprised if the bank manager we are imagining addressed them with "Hi ya sweetheart" or "Yo!" or if she asked them about whom they were dating or told them about the feud between her uncle and the owner of the bakery in her hometown. While some customers might enjoy the unexpected conversations of the bank manager, it is likely that many would find this conversation unusually eccentric or even inappropriate and would draw some conclusions about the bank manager's personality or consider her gossip to be frivolous or distracting.

Interestingly, however, in spite of the topics raised in this unanticipated and possibly distracting conversation, only if the bank manager's language lacked certain structural conventions of standardized English would customers or coworkers draw conclusions about the manager's level of education, conclusions that may or may not be accurate. Expectations about language structure in settings where standarized English is usually heard may be even more powerful than expectations about appropriate content. A missing article ("Please sign paper") or subject-verb disagreement ("Your money are now transferred") will not prevent a listener from understanding the speaker's meaning, yet these "errors" tend to call greater negative attention to a speaker than the insertion of regional slang or an informal greeting.

Expectations About Correctness

If the most significant purpose of the language of wider communication is, indeed, to communicate, and if communication is not actually hindered by the way verbs are formed ("Your money are now transferred"), then why do some people hold such judgmental expectations about grammatical or structural correctness? And, moreover, why are these expectations so powerful?

One answer to these questions has to do with the way all languages change over time. As English, Spanish, Cambodian, Mandarin, and other languages evolved through centuries of use, they not only developed a vocabulary that has changed and expanded but also developed a characteristic set of relationships among words, what is called *syntax*. Among English speakers, sentences are expected to have nouns and verbs; verbs are declined or changed according to when the action in the sentence occurred: "I *am going* to the mall today" versus "I *went* to the mall last week." But this is not the case in all languages. Some languages indicate tense by the context of the situation, leaving the verb itself unchanged. Some do not require separate verbs at all, since the nouns carry with them an implied action. Furthermore, linguistic descriptions like that done on African American English by William Labov (1972) explain that dialects of English each have their own rules of grammar and usage, and what sounds correct in one dialect may sound incorrect in another. For example, double negatives are correct in many languages, including African American English. Hearing a dialect with this grammatical usage within the context of a setting in which a language of wider communication is more common, listeners may feel they have heard incorrect Standard English rather than correct dialect usage.

That languages vary suggests that their everyday use has pushed each one in a specific direction that has resulted in highly distinctive and individualistic qualities. Over time, as we have mentioned, the most widely accepted language structures, those of wider communication, most often are those used by speakers who have the highest professional standing or the most economic influence. The connection between dialects and the social standing of their speakers, rather than issues of communication difficulty, may account for the negative response nonstandard usage often receives.

The more each one of us knows about the history of English language and the social dimensions of language use, the less likely we are to form negative judgments about speakers based on their dialects. Nonetheless, listeners notice if nonstandard usage occurs when the language of wider communication is expected, and they conclude that the error has been made either because the speaker has not assimilated the conventions set by the dominant group or because he or she has chosen not to switch codes in the expected way.

Making such conventional "errors" unintentionally, speakers may unwittingly create bias against themselves, as the listener makes this into an opportunity to make a judgment about the speaker and, in this way, assert authority. On the other hand, speakers may make such an "error" intentionally, purposely setting themselves against the dominant group by dressing in a culturally identifying way and speaking in a manner most familiar to their community groups. Individuals then accentuate the difference and distance between themselves and their listeners. This could be done to demonstrate or re-create, for the listeners, the alienation the speaker feels or to isolate and celebrate the speaker's identity.

 Reflection
Sharing Memories About Misused Conventions

Think of times in your life when you either intentionally or accidentally misused the expected set of conventions when you were speaking. This misuse could have occurred in formal settings with large audiences or intimate settings with small audiences. Jot down a word or phrase to stand for these stories. Share some of these stories with a classmate in a face-to-face or email exchange. Find out as many details as possible about each other's stories. Then, for this reflection, write about how your stories are alike or different and what observations they lead you to make about misused and misusing conventions.

Social Implications

We have touched on a number of complex social issues connected to the use of the language of wider communication in the United States. As professors of Composition who have studied writing development and language use, in terms of college writing, we can see no communicative superiority to the conventions of standardized English over those of other dialects. As we mentioned earlier, linguists have found no one dialect that more effectively allows for the full range of language expression than any other dialect. But we also see little indication that the conventions of other dialects are soon to be considered appropriate for most college writing. In order to focus readers' attention more closely on the content of the writing and away from unexpected uses of syntax and word choice, college writers are expected to edit the final versions of their papers specifically for the conventions of standardized English.

Consequently, it is reassuring to note that in our experience we have found that college students who are speakers of various dialects become proficient code switchers by giving attention to a relatively few conventions—those that we identify in the editing chapter of this text. This switching does require conscious attention and may make the process of preparing a final version of an essay more time-consuming than it might otherwise be, although our own experience as writers leads us to believe that editing is always time-consuming. For writers, unlike speakers, can take time, and are expected to take time, to adjust the way they present their material to their audience.

CHAPTER 4

A Map of College Writing

Reading and Writing for Essays 3 and 4

Locating Yourself in the History of College Writing

Now that we have reflected on language communities and the language of wider communication, we will more directly focus on the language community of American college writing that you have recently entered. In this chapter we ask you to consider ways in which your own history has intersected with this community, a community that extends well beyond your own college campus to colleges, universities, and academic organizations across the country. The history of college writing is not a chronology of events that has already ended; rather, it is part of a continuing story involving writing courses, exams, standards, and expectations—all of which exert influence on you and every other student currently enrolled in a college writing course. Much of what may seem arbitrary or mysterious about college writing, and your relationship to it, can be explained by this larger, public history that has impacted the form and content of contemporary college writing courses, as well as all of our beliefs about what it means to be a college writer.

As we remarked earlier, because you are taking a college writing class, you have probably been told stories of past writing classes by roommates, friends at other schools, or even parents and grandparents. While it may seem from these stories that college writing courses have been around since the time of the cave dwellers, until the late nineteenth century, no writing courses, and certainly no college writing requirements, existed in the United States. The closest a college student might have come to taking a writing course would have been a course in rhetoric and exposition, a class more like a present-day speech class than one in writing.

The Beginnings of College Writing in America

From the work of historians such as James Berlin (1987), John Brereton (1995), Robert Connors (1997), Tom Fox (1999), and Albert Kitzhaber (1990), we find the changing profile of American colleges—their purposes, students, and faculty. The first American colleges and universities, particularly the elite, private universities, were built to provide higher education for young men of the wealthy upper class, students whose college careers had, most likely, been selected for them long before they entered grammar and preparatory school. By the mid-nineteenth century, the middle-class population of the United States had become more socially and economically diverse. Immigrants were arriving from Europe and elsewhere, and the country's economy was becoming increasingly industry based, allowing more Americans to earn middle-class incomes. More colleges were built to accommodate the increasing numbers of young people who could afford higher education. As a result, the population of students on college campuses was gradually becoming more diverse; college students included not only men from wealthy economic and social backgrounds, who, in a sense, had been preparing for college all their lives, but also young men (and some women) from the growing middle class of Americans, individuals who had not been trained in private schools and social clubs.

As the student population changed, so too did the language experiences that students brought to the university. While all the students at American universities spoke English, they did not all speak in the same dialect or register. Some had, throughout their lives, become used to hearing and speaking standard, formal constructions; others had grown up hearing a mix of formal constructions and slang or street language. The conventional King's English of the wealthy class that had been the norm for entering freshmen was mixing with the more everyday language or vernacular English of the middle class. Faculty and administrators, themselves part of the social elite, were concerned about this apparent lack of standardized spoken and written English among students. In 1874, partially in response to these changing demographics and the perceived needs of a more diverse student body, the president of Harvard University began the designs for English A, a course that was soon to become the first required course at Harvard and the most influential writing course in the country.

---

13 Reflection
Your Place in College Writing History

As we have tried to suggest, any one individual's experience with college writing is influenced by centuries of personal and public history. For this reflection, write about where these two evolving histories of college writing intersect for you. Locate yourself and your family history in the evolution of college writing within the American college system. In the 1870s, when Harvard instituted English A, what language or languages were your ancestors speaking and where were they living? To what extent and in what ways do you imagine writing was a part of their daily life?

The Evolution of College Writing

The diversity of students enrolled at universities in the late nineteenth century is slight compared with the diversity of today. Those faculty who were dismayed by the prevalence of vernacular English among students more than a century ago would surely be surprised were they to walk across a contemporary college campus, hearing not only the many dialects of English but also any number of different languages spoken by students from a broad range of cultural backgrounds. They would be similarly surprised were they to listen in on contemporary college writing classes and hear the way college writing is now described.

The relatively singular vision of college writing that existed in American universities in the 1800s, what Robert Connors referred to as "one great force" (1997, 69) was, in large part, a reflection of the equally singular set of beliefs and values shared by early college faculty. But as student populations became increasingly diverse, faculty gradually diversified as well. White, male instructors were joined by men and women from a range of ethnicities and cultures with diverse personal and professional experiences and philosophies. This "evolutionary change" (102) in the makeup of college faculty, which continues today, necessarily influenced what students were learning and broadened the question of what they were expected to know. College writing, like colleges themselves, began to undergo a process of change. It was no longer possible, and it can be argued that it was no longer desirable, to find a single, monolithic definition of college writing.

These changes in how college writing is defined have been reinforced and validated by changes in our understanding of what it means to write. When universities first began accepting students from a wider range of social and economic backgrounds, English A and courses at other universities modeled after English A were designed for the purpose of standardizing students' writing. It was assumed that there was a single, correct way to write (and speak) that required mastery of specific forms and phrasings that were already familiar to the upper class. Instructors concentrated their effort and students' attention on the production of daily themes, first used by Barrett Wendell at Harvard, that were written on assigned subjects, often without revising and with few readers' comments along the way.

The influence of American cultural diversity on college writing, along with teaching experiences and research in the discipline of Composition that coalesced in the 1960s, provides evidence that writing is much more complicated than the production of a daily theme and attention to sentence correctness would suggest. Lester Faigley (1986), James Moffett (1987), Sondra Perl (1979), Nancy Sommers (1980), and other scholars who study how people write have collected evidence to demonstrate that writing is not simply the act of recording completed ideas that have been stored in our heads. Writing is a creative process, one that takes place over time and is influenced by a vast number of experiences and reader reactions. Readers see the final product, the finished text of writing, but what it took to produce that text is, in large part, invisible. We can find evidence of a writer's creative process in the visible form of drafts and notes. Yet most of the evolution of a piece of writing remains invisible in the thoughts and feelings that occurred as the writer produced his or her work.

Traditionally, the final product has received all of the attention of writing instruction. Yet the larger part of writing, what takes place on the way to producing a finished text, holds the most influence over one's development as a writer and begins long before one sits down to work on a particular task, long before one enters college. Consider, for example, the relationship between the language or languages you spoke before entering college and the language you are expected to use in the classroom. Let's say you learned to speak English after years of speaking Spanish or Tagalog or Vietnamese in your home with your parents and siblings; this will, by necessity, influence the way you hear American academic language and what you feel about college writing in English. If your first language is English, you did not learn it in the context of a university, with all the expectations and qualifications that come with writing for a college professor. Whatever languages you speak and write, you have also had personal experiences with learning and textbooks and classrooms and teachers that influence—in positive and negative ways—any writing that you produce.

---

14 Reflection
Finding Similarities and Differences in Writers' Experiences

With one other person in class, exchange responses to Reflection 13, or read them aloud to each other. Once you have listened to or read each other's writing, write about what the other person has written, about the way his or her experience strikes you as familiar or not. How is it like or unlike your own experience? What surprised or confused you? Tell the writer your reactions, feelings, and thoughts about the experience he or she described. Be sure to exchange one more time so that you can read the response you have written to each other's original entry.

Negotiating College Writing Standards

At this point, you may be skeptical about the picture of college writing that we have been outlining. Our claim that there is no longer a single standard for college writing and that your own personal and cultural experience should powerfully influence your writing may contradict your own experience and the very fact that you may be required to take your present writing course. Although college writing and our understanding of it have evolved in the ways we have described, college writing does continue to be influenced by its origins as a means of achieving uniformity and standardization. You may know from firsthand experience that colleges do, indeed, create standards and maintain expectations for their students. Writing placement tests that students take before coming to campus or soon after, writing achievement or exit exams that occur before graduation, and required and recommended writing courses provide evidence that college faculty continue to expect students to write in a particular way. And because tests and requirements vary from college to college, it is clear that expectations vary, that what is valued on one campus may not seem to be what is valued elsewhere.

Just as your college has developed its curricular requirements over time—through months or even years of faculty discussion and debate—it also developed a set of values about student writing, about how writing should be measured and taught, about what forms of writing should be emphasized. As the writing requirements and curriculum at your school evolved, faculty had to answer questions like these: How many writing courses should be required? How should placement in writing courses be determined? What kinds of courses should be available—expository, creative writing, autobiography? Should students receive academic credit or grades for writing courses? Answers to these questions and to other questions specific to your school indicate that while college writing now has a much broader definition than it had in the 1870s, the tradition of creating and maintaining standards continues, even as it is significantly influenced by cultural diversity and individual creativity. Indeed, one of the reasons we had for writing this book was to help students negotiate the demands of college writing standards and requirements, using, to your advantage, what we have come to know about the nature of writing and the development of writing abilities.

---

15 Reflection
Writing Requirements at Your School

Find out what are the writing requirements of your school. List these requirements and make a corresponding list of how you found out about these requirements and your school's writing courses. Draw some conclusions about what seem to be the standards and expectations for college writing at your school.

Writing Outside of the English Department or Writing Program

The expectations and standards that we have described so far develop inside English departments or writing programs and university curriculum committees. But there are other parts of the university that will affect you as a writer, if they have not already. Each discipline at a university—each area of research and teaching—has its own set of writing standards called *conventions*. As you recall, we used the term *conventions* earlier to describe the particular features of close-to-home language communities. In the context of academic disciplines, writing conventions apply to a range of concerns, from small, sentence-level issues to larger issues about essay structure, to an even larger concern with what subjects are worth writing about. For example, conventions vary from discipline to discipline about the use of the first person (*I*), the value of passive voice ("The investigator argues" or "I argue" versus "It is argued by the investigator"), the use of abstracts or summaries at either the beginning or the end of a piece of writing, the value of citing current sources, historical facts, or newly created experiences. As with the general writing standards set by your school, these more specialized conventions have evolved after years of discussion and debate. They are closely tied to the nature of a particular discipline and to what professionals in each field value intellectually. In fact, this tie is so close that when individual members of a discipline refocus their attention and reevaluate their scholarly practices, two things happen. First, established disciplines enlarge or change their conventions. Second, when the refocusing is too significant, new or subdisciplines evolve with new sets of writing conventions: psychology splits into cognitive and behavioral; sociology divides into quantitative analysis and qualitative analysis; English Studies becomes literature and composition.

Reflection
Writing Conventions in Other Courses

Write about the writing that is expected in other courses you are taking. Recollect and record some current or past experiences with writing essays or reports in college courses outside of those that focus, like this one, specifically on writing. What are some of the conventions that you are or were expected to follow? What were the expectations about the length, the style of citations, the bibliography, the use of particular kinds of information, and so on? How did you come to know what was expected?

Connecting Personal Style to Disciplinary Conventions

What happens when a writer's personal style, one shaped by a lifetime of personal writing experiences, cultural influences, and creative tastes, meets up with the conventions and expectations of college writing in a variety of disciplines? Sometimes a writer's stylistic preferences and the conventions of a discipline fit nicely together: a tendency for writing long, complex sentences that include lots of highly descriptive illustrations and repeat one's main points may be a style that adapts comfortably to a literature assignment. But the same style may conflict loudly with the conventions of a scientific report, where sentences are expected to be brief, illustrations concise, and repetitions deleted.

While it is not necessary or desirable for writers to strip themselves of their particular preferences in terms of writing style, it is useful to develop a sharpened awareness of which stylistic features they seem to favor most and, at the same time, to become familiar with the expected or favored conventions of the various disciplines in which they are asked to complete writing assignments. With such knowledge, writers are more likely to notice how their own stylistic preferences connect to and perhaps complement the general features of disciplinary style. They are more likely to notice, also, ways in which they might need to modify their style for writing in particular academic disciplines.

 Reflection
Disciplinary Writing Conventions and Personal Style

Write about the relationship between your own style of writing and what seems to be expected in college. Recall one or several courses in which you were asked to write essays or reports, and recall the expected conventions of this writing; it might be useful to draw from one of the courses you focused on in the last reflection. Did the conventions seem to fit comfortably with your way of writing? How did you feel that you had to adapt your own writing style to the conventions? How successful were you? How did you determine this success?

What, Then, Is College Writing?

College writing continues to change and although it varies conventionally from discipline to discipline, college writing does have two invariably identifiable features: it is *explicit*, that is, it spells out a particular focus or point of view or position, and second, college writing is *reflective*, that is, it analyzes or interprets a chosen material, text, experience, or phenomenon.

Contrast these features with those expected in creative writing. The focus or point of a story or poem is intended to be implicit rather than explicit. Writers of stories and poems work to structure their texts with multiple layers of meaning. The fiction writer presents a story, shows what happened, and then readers go about analyzing what it means. The poet presents images and language that represent experience and then readers can spell out their possible interpretations.

An academic text may use stories or images as well. But the academic essay does the interpreting for the reader. Indeed, analysis is the primary focus of an academic essay. The academic writer presents material and then tells us what to make of it, how to interpret it, and what it means. Whatever subject a college writer addresses, he or she not only records information or tells what happened but also *reflects on* and *analyzes* the material presented. It is this reflective attention that may be said to be the intellectual work of academic writing. In the process of determining which kind of information is most valuable and then analyzing that information, the writer figures out what he or she has to say and how to say it. The focus writers select may depend on their personal interest in a particular topic, the audience being addressed, or externally imposed requirements or limitations. In an academic essay, the writer must make this focus evident to the reader and then provide relevant information so that readers know exactly where the writer stands, what position he or she is taking, and what specific points he or she is making.

CHAPTER
5

Your Own Experience as a Writer

Reading and Writing for Essays 3 and 4

Looking Back and Looking Ahead

Now that we have described to you the social and institutional history of college writing, we will discuss how to find your place in this community of college writing and how to do so in such a way that your writing is not just correct but also unique to you. While writing successfully is contingent on your use of expected conventions, it is also contingent upon your ability to make your writing distinct and personally recognizable. For although there are generalizable qualities of college writing, each essay is also marked by the individual voice of the writer, a voice that emerges from the writer's stance or position in relation to the subject of the essay intersecting with the writer's collective personal experience and the knowledge gathered through these experiences. The reflective and analytical writing you do in this chapter will lead you to this intersection and help you to define your own writer's voice.

---

18 Reflection
Remembering First Experiences with Writing in College

Write about the first essay or writing assignment you had in college—it may have been the one assigned in this book or one that you did for a different course. Use some or all of these questions to prompt your reflection: How did you feel about writing this assignment? How comfortable did you feel with the words as you were putting them together?

Did you feel differently about this assignment from the way you felt about the writing assignments you completed in high school? How would you characterize the tone of voice you were using? How confident were you about the essay when you handed it in to your instructor?

Taking a Stance: The Sound of Your Voice in Your Writing

Having read this far in *Writing Your Way Through College*, you probably have a good sense of our author voices—our tone, the formality of our language, and the general patterns of our syntax. When you first began this book, it's likely that you opened it with certain expectations about how it would read—after all, it *is* a textbook, not a novel or a popular magazine. The voices that greeted you may or may not have met your expectations.

The choices we made about the voice for this book were conscious ones based on the genre in which we are working, that of a college composition textbook, our specific goals for the book, and the information we are presenting. Let us take you inside our thinking about these choices for a moment, to serve as an example of how writers develop their voice. If you look back at Chapter 1, for instance, you may notice that our tone in that chapter is much like the one you might expect to hear from a teacher on the first day of class; we are a bit formal as we outline the purposes of the book and give some idea about what you can expect. Similarly, on the first day of class, we, like most teachers, try to outline what the course will focus on during the semester, what the assignments are, what books to buy. Usually, we have our students write a little during the initial meeting to get started. On the first day, we keep at bay the fact that all of us—students and teachers—are unique individuals with complex lives. We disregard the fact that talking about something is a pale and often distorted shadow of doing it. We talk, instead, in that generic way teachers do, a way that seems to assume that all the students in their classes are alike and need to hear the same thing.

Since the purpose of that first chapter was to introduce the book and convince you of its value and authority, we sometimes let the book do the talking, writing phrases like "*This book* can help you see yourself . . ." and "*This book* provides an insider's view. . . ." We put the book, rather than ourselves, in a place of authority in these instances, attempting to establish the significance of the text you were about to read. This kind of phrasing has the advantage of establishing authority by keeping the writer's individuality obscured but, as a result, can create some peculiar language. It leads the writer into passive rather than active constructions: "*This* textbook asks you to read about college writing," as if the textbook wrote itself and is now giving you assignments.

To take a particular stance and find the words and organization to create a corresponding voice, writers rely on their personal histories and past experiences. As writers of this text, for example, we are teachers who, after many years of experience, have become comfortable with both the college writing we assign and the formal, professional version of college writing that is called *academic discourse*. We are also generally approachable, friendly teachers who tend to present to students a personal side as well as the professional. In writing the introductory chapter, we chose to take a stance that would combine the two sides, leaning slightly more toward the formal and professional. That is, we wrote in our most teacherly, professional voice, one that seems neutral and somewhat distant, and in a way that we hoped would sound authoritative but not intimidating. Here are two versions of a passage from Chapter 1:

Version 1

A final myth about college writing is that it is something you can take in a semester or two and get over with quickly. The writing placement exams and discretely defined writing requirements at many colleges falsely suggest that writing can be mastered once and for all before you enter college or by the end of a specific course or two. You may have the impression that one need only learn a particular format or some new vocabulary in order for the difficulties of college writing to be resolved.

Version 2

Finally, many of you may believe that college writing is something you can get out of the way in a semester or two. As teachers, we're concerned that by using writing placement exams and specific writing requirements, administrators of college writing programs give you the false idea that writing can be mastered once and for all either before you come to college or in a couple of courses. By creating such requirements, we teachers and administrators may be giving you the impression that if you learn a particular structure or formula or add some new vocabulary, you will solve all your difficulties of writing at college.

Notice that in version 1 you exist, but we don't seem to be there. In this version, we constructed the sentences so that the placement exams and writing requirements—not human beings—appear to be responsible for any beliefs you may have. As the writers, we remain very distant from the concepts we are describing. By contrast, in version 2, we not only exist, but are personally engaged with the concepts we are describing ("we're concerned"), and we become identified among the group of teachers and administrators who institute the exams and requirements that may be giving the wrong impression of college writing.

The differences between the two versions are subtle, and there is nothing wrong with either one. Although you may have personal preferences, one version is not inherently better than the other. Rather, we, the authors, have presented ourselves differently in each one. The audience for whom a piece of writing is intended, the purpose for which the writing is created, and the way the writer wishes to present him or herself affect the writer's choice of what stance seems most appropriate to take for a given writing situation. In this passage, our goal was to gain the trust of our readers, for you to hear us as primarily knowledgeable authorities and secondarily as friendly, experienced teachers, so version 1 appears in the text.

Writers have a lifetime of experiences on which to draw when placing themselves in what they write and taking a stance in writing. Unless writers take the opportunity to identify and reflect on these experiences and to use them in their writing, they are likely to shortchange themselves, their writing, and their readers. For instance, when we selected a teacherly, professional stance and its corresponding tone of voice, we did so because of the audience for whom we were writing (students in college writing classes) and our purpose (to introduce our textbook), and we drew on those related parts of our lives in order to create that stance in an authentic, believable way. After the text progresses, and even later in that first chapter, we draw on other parts of our history as teachers and writers, shifting our stance and the voice in which we are writing to one that, we expect, is slightly less distant than the one you hear at the beginning of the book.

Reflection
Writing for Different Audiences

Return to the first reflection in Chapter 1, in which you wrote about your expectations and fears for your writing class. Imagine that the person who coordinates the writing courses at your college or university wants to get a better understanding of students' perceptions of writing and has asked students to write a letter to him or her about their fears and expectations as they begin the term. Rewrite the first reflection in a way that would be desirable and appropriate for responding to this request. While this writing situation, its audience and purpose, requires a different voice from what you used in the original entry, the writing still comes from you and draws on the same experiences and perspective as the first reflection.

When you are done with the letter, place it next to the piece you wrote for Reflection 1. Make some notes about how the two are alike and different. What words, stylistic features, sentence structures, and so forth distinguish one from the other and help to create the two different stances or voices?

Taking a Stance: Identifying the Perspective from Which You Begin

Finding an appropriate voice for your writing is intimately tied to the perspective you take on a subject and on yourself as a writer. That is, taking a stance in college writing means identifying how you see yourself as a writer and, in particular, as a writer of college essays. It means being comfortable with and knowledgeable about this point of view—using it to your advantage to create a strong, honest voice.

So, it is useful to examine your own connections to college writing. In Chapter 4, we describe some of the features of college writing, calling that chapter "a map of college writing." Extending that metaphor of location, let us examine college writing as if it were a new city you were moving into where you found a map, like the ones found in shopping malls or state parks, with an arrow pointing to your present location, marked "You are here." Just as you would look at your location on a map in relation to what was surrounding you, we would like you to think about yourself as a writer in relation to the history and evolution of college writing: Where are you in these surroundings of college writing? What do you see from where you are standing? What writing situations have you found yourself in previously?

To find your location in writing, consider both your past and present situations. You have already written on your hopes, fears, and expectations about *college* writing and *college* textbooks. You can also recall and record your past writing experiences, experiences that started the moment you began to use written language to hold and shape your ideas. You have been a writer outside of school (at home, at work, in the community) and a writer in school (in classes, at meetings, and where you live).

Writing experiences, the ones that you remember most vividly, influence what you now believe to be true about writing and about yourself as a writer. Ultimately, such experiences shape your assumptions and attitudes toward college writing and your sense of your own writing abilities. Losing the poetry award in third grade to your best friend, suffering through an impossibly demanding eighth-grade teacher, learning the responsibility of contributing to the school paper—as experiences like these accumulate over time, they affect us in ways we may not immediately be aware of. Predominantly positive experiences will have one kind of effect, which may be obscured or even wiped out by one or two especially painful experiences.

Recalling Writing Experiences

To illustrate how past writing experiences can shape current thoughts about writing and learning to write and to illustrate how writers recall and analyze their own experiences, one of us has written out three recollected experiences that could provide information and evidence for an academic essay. You will notice as you read the passages that the voice in which they are written shifts dramatically from what you are used to hearing in *Writing Your Way Through College*. This shift in voice occurs because in these passages we are telling stories rather than providing information, analysis, and advice. The subject matter of most of this textbook and of nearly all academic writing demands a more distant voice than the voice of a storyteller.

Recalling past events can be easier if the process begins with a list of words or phrases that come to mind as you think of events in your life related to writing or learning to write. A list like this is written in a kind of code, not intended to be meaningful to anyone other than the writer. But it is important to recognize that this list *is* writing, the first writing to recollect something from personal writing experiences. From this list, a few events will stand out as being more vivid, more memorable, and, consequently, more easily recorded at the present time. As you read the three following recollections, keep in mind that considered together, they provide a place from which the person who remembered them is likely to draw some assumptions or conclusions about writing and learning to write.

Experience 1

In seventh grade I learned that I could not *just be* a writer. I don't remember how it happened that I wanted to be a writer, or why. It's likely that I came into Westlake Junior High in Oakland, California, thinking of myself as a writer, already. I know that I had been answering the question "What do you want to be when you grow up?" with "A writer" for several years before I learned that this was not an acceptable answer. Mrs. Donaldson, the physical education teacher in whose presence I felt even more clumsy and skinny than I felt at all times during junior high, enlightened me. "You can't just be a writer," she responded when I took my turn to tell the career I'd chosen on seventh-grade career day. "You have to have talent." Years later it occurred to me that Mrs. Donaldson believed not only that writing abilities are impossible to develop but that it was possible to tell, perhaps from the way I stumbled at gymnastics, that I had no talent as a writer. I learned her lesson well enough to never again say I wanted to be a writer, not even after I was publishing and, in at least some people's eyes, becoming one.

Experience 2

All through junior high and high school, I avoided sports whenever I could. It wasn't until I was in college that I started swimming, and not until I left college that I discovered I could run. On my twenty-seventh birthday, I ran twenty-seven miles. Just before my twenty-eighth birthday, I broke my leg skiing so I didn't run twenty-eight—or any—miles. In fact, the twenty-seven-mile run was, and looks likely to remain, a one-time-only event. However, I can't resist saying, I got a lot of mileage out of that run. I published a poem about it, "The Center of a 27-Mile Run," in a local newspaper. For some reason, the production editor of the newspaper had extra copies of that issue, two hundred of them, which he gave to me. I cut the poem out of about twenty copies and sent it to friends. Eventually I used the newspapers as packing material, boxes of dishes, glasses, photographs packed with layers of newspaper containing my poem. And, sad to say, a lot of newspapers were thrown out. I thought of packing up boxes of the newspapers to move them too, but I didn't do it.

Experience 3

Sometime in the middle of fifth grade, probably around Veterans Day, the school district sponsored an essay contest on the theme of patriotism. Rather than letting those students who were interested volunteer to write an entry, my English teacher, Mrs. Collins, required that we each write one, and then she would select the one to be submitted to the contest. Seeing myself as a writer, I invested a great deal of time and emotion into my essay. I thought carefully about each line, trying to imagine the heartfelt reaction that each one would create in my reader. My essay was, in fact, selected by the teacher to represent the class. But before it was submitted to the school district committee, Mrs. Collins asked me to meet with her after school so that she could help me make some revisions. I sat in a chair next to my teacher, watching her cross out words and phrases with a red pen and write in new words directly over the words of my essay. With each change, she said, "There, don't you think that's better?" She did not seem to notice that I did not agree. I said nothing but I did feel angry and embarrassed. I don't know what happened to the essay after that, though I know that my mother put the award letter I got in a special box on the bookcase.

---

20 | **Reflection**
Drawing Conclusions from Writing Experiences

Based on these experiences from her life, what assumptions or conclusions do you imagine the writer would make about writing, learning to write, or being a writer? List three assumptions that might evolve for the writer from these experiences, identifying the parts of her recorded experiences from which she might draw these conclusions.

Using Recollections as Evidence from Which to Make Assumptions

Just as you did in the previous reflection, the author of these experiences herself could analyze the events and her reactions in order to understand her current perspective on writing and learning to write. The recollected experiences become the data or evidence that provides an explanation for why the writer now feels as she does and can begin to provide her with a sense of her own perspective on writing and learning to write and how she came to hold that perspective.

---

21 Reflection
Writing from Your Own History as a Writer

First write out a list of experiences in your life as a writer, a student of writing, or a student in general—let your mind carry you back as far as it can, moving from your earliest to your most recent experiences with writing. Use fragments or code words so that you can concentrate on searching your memories, not on creating a well-crafted list. Choose three of these experiences. Record what you can remember of each of these experiences.

---

22 Reflection
Drawing Conclusions About Others from Their Writing Experiences

Exchange with a classmate the experiences you wrote about in Reflection 21. Then, as you did in Reflection 20 with the experiences we included, look at your classmate's recorded experiences for connections, and identify some of the assumptions and attitudes that you imagine your classmate could have about writing, about him or herself as a writer, about learning to write, or about learning. What events or comments in the narrative have led you to these conclusions? Share your observations with one another so that you can get an idea about what your own experiences suggest to others about you. When you are done, read one another's reflection and write a few sentences about how the reflection fits or does not fit with your own sense of yourself.

Since it can be difficult for us to look at ourselves with an unbiased eye, in the last reflection we asked you to have a classmate use your writing to draw conclusions about your assumptions and attitudes toward learning, being a student, and being a student of writing. The conclusions he or she recorded may have matched your own thinking about yourself or may have varied wildly from what you think. How closely they matched your own analysis depends, in part, on the evidence that was provided by the experiences you wrote out. Your classmate could rely only on those experiences and the way you told them as evidence, and he or she made generalizations about you based on that evidence. On the other hand, you have a whole lifetime of evidence—experiences, feelings, and thoughts—to draw from. If the experiences you selected to write about were representative of the larger body of evidence that you carry with you, then chances are good that the conclusions presented by you and by your classmate were very similar. As we suggested at the beginning of this chapter, successful college writing results from the comfortable intersection between the history we bring to our writing and the subject on which we must write. In the last two reflections, you had a chance to find out how comfortably you were able to make that intersection.

CHAPTER

6

Navigating the Conventions of Speaking and Writing

Reading and Writing for Essays 5 and 6

What More Is There to Learn About College Writing?

One of your challenges, as a college writer, is to identify and develop a perspective you can offer on any particular topic that makes your voice heard and your words understood by readers. So far, we have been describing how college writers learn to situate themselves in relation to the college writing community, as one would do in any new language setting. We have also considered how the topics and style a writer chooses are influenced by cultural traditions and communication conventions that shift from one setting to the next and by a writer's own understanding of the writing process and past writing experiences and expectations. But how are language conventions learned and used?

The distinction between spoken and written language has been widely explored in a variety of disciplines, including composition, philosophy, psychology, and linguistics (see, for example, Elbow 1985, Kroll and Vann 1981, Ong 1982, and Scribner and Cole 1981). In this chapter, we draw on these distinctions so as to make clearer the process by which humans learn language conventions. First, we focus on the more familiar medium of speaking and, then, on writing in general. Finally, we turn to the conventions characteristic of college or academic communities, the conventions that will have the most direct effect on what you choose to say as well as how you choose to present yourself to the instructors in your college courses.

Jot down notions about writing and language that seem important to you as a result of the writing course you are currently taking. What have you learned so far about language and writing that is most significant to you as a student? What did you read, write, or talk about during this course that has led you to your current understanding?

Learning the Conventions as a Speaker

As we discussed in Chapters 2 and 3, establishing the confidence and authority to speak within one's family, within communities one enters or joins, or within the world of wider communication depends largely on learning the cultural and personal traditions that affect these language communities—issues such as authority hierarchies, gender roles, sibling positions, and so forth. In the course of learning these traditions, one also learns language conventions—what is appropriate to say, when, how, and to whom. This is not a matter of learning what is right or wrong, but what is *conventional* and expected. But how does such learning occur? Family members don't sit you down and have you take notes from a lecture about language conventions; the groups you join don't hand out a list of acceptable language traditions.

You learn many of these traditions and the conventions that derive from them without even trying to, without knowing you are doing so. As a member of a family, you are immediately integrated into its traditions, learning to speak in the context of that particular family and in relation to the conventions that have grown from its history. You learn that if you use certain words in certain situations you can expect certain results: cursing at dinner may result in your being asked to leave or in shared laughter; yelling in order to get someone's attention may get a helpful response from the other end of the house or a reprimand from your grandmother. Similarly, outside the family, without necessarily thinking about it, you watch people interact with one another. You listen to the words they use, their tone, the subjects they discuss, and then you try out comparable language in your own conversations.

Individual experiences and the lessons of trial and error teach us other conventions. When the way you speak achieves positive results, you may respond by trying to repeat this language behavior or something about it. For instance, once you have a job interview and are hired as a result, you may try to recall some of what you said or how you said it the next time you interview for a job. Getting a friendly response when you talk with someone you have just met encourages you to approach others in a similar way. Likewise, negative results can often lead to changes in language behaviors. After your mother cautions, "Don't use those words in this house!" you may try to respect her wishes. Having been unable to convince your boss to let you have the day off one week, you will likely try a new approach the next time you ask.

Many of the conventions of spoken language, then, are learned in a relatively passive manner—by continued exposure to them or by positive and negative rewards that either reinforce behaviors or cause you to change them.

But as you move farther away from the known context of family, friends, and familiar situations, into more distant circles of communication, conventions of speech can become more complex and difficult to learn, and you may need to give active attention to learning what is appropriate and effective. Consider the following contrast. At home, you may want to convince a younger sister to do some chores for you. Your success in getting what you want depends, in part, on how well you express yourself to her—how well you know and use the conventions of brother-sister or sister-sister talk. Do you threaten her or use reason? Do you mention incidents from the past or stick only to the present? Most likely, the passive lessons of trial and error, of past observations and experience, will provide the answers to such questions.

Now, imagine that you are new to a job; you are trying to convince a coworker to take some of your scheduled hours so you can go to a concert. Again, your success depends in part on your understanding and use of appropriate conventions. Though you may have had the automatic or entitled authority of an older sibling at home, what authority do you claim at work? What are the expectations about who can ask for time off—only older employees? Only those with several months' experience? Only the boss' nephew? You may be able to figure out some of these conventions through observing other employees and gaining experience. But trial-and-error methods for learning conventions don't always work; in fact, the more unusual and less frequently displayed conventions may not be apparent until a seasoned employee takes you aside and explains them to you.

The difficulty of learning conventions through trial and error becomes even more pronounced in increasingly distant communication situations. Imagine you are at a store in the mall, trying to convince someone that the store overcharged you for an item you bought last week. What traditions surround this conversation? To whom is it appropriate to speak—the sales clerk, the manager, or an off-site billing agency? Should you demand a refund or politely question the store's accuracy? Again, you may be able to learn about this unique language situation through trial and error, but it could be to your immediate financial advantage to ask someone in advance, perhaps a friend who has had a similar problem or someone who works at a different store.

An interesting point is that when you learn the conventions, you are not learning what is correct everywhere but what is most usual in a specific language situation, what is *conventional* and expected. In this scenario, it may be that the store manager handles inquiries like yours. It would not be *wrong* to ask a sales clerk, but doing so would be less likely to get you the result you are seeking, because it would not be the expected language behavior for that setting.

So far, our discussion of conventions has addressed two aspects of communication at once: *rhetorical conventions* and *usage conventions*. The broader rhetorical conventions concern what is usually expected or appropriate to talk about in different settings, to different listeners, whereas usage conventions concern how it is appropriate to speak, what words and phrasing are acceptable. Again, in familiar situations, you are less likely to think about either rhetorical or usage conventions. With close friends, you usually feel free to talk about anything in any way you choose. In other situations, especially when you are new to a communication context, both rhetorical conventions and usage conventions may require your conscious attention.

---

24 Reflection
Identifying and Learning Community Conventions

First, select one of the communities, groups, or organizations that you are connected to at college—this could be a formal organization such as a student club or team, or a more informal setting such as a classroom-related or self-selected study group, a campus residence group, or a group formed around a particular interest. Next, identify and make a list of some of this community's language conventions: the kinds of topics you expect to hear, which individuals are usually included in the conversation, how you would describe the kind of language that is used, and so forth. Finally, write about how you and other members of the community learned these conventions—whom did you watch, with whom did you speak, or what did you read in order to come to know about and understand them?

Learning the Conventions as a Writer

Like speakers, writers also must understand the traditions of the particular language situation and the resulting rhetorical and usage conventions. In some cases, the differences between spoken and written language conventions are minimal, making the transition quite simple. Writing a letter or email to your parents may be no more agonizing than speaking to them. But sometimes the conventions of writing can feel alien, particularly in those cases where writing is the only accepted means of communication and, therefore, you have no familiar conventions from speech on which to draw.

Furthermore, learning these conventions for writing may be more difficult than for speaking. The same ways of learning traditions and conventions for speaking—gathering information from what you see and experience, from observation, and from trial and error—are available for learning written conventions, but they are not always as helpful. First, we talk a lot more than we write, so speech is constantly present in our lives in a way that writing is not. And second, since we don't write as often as we speak, there are fewer opportunities to gain experience in writing; consequently, the most common approach for learning speech conventions, trial and error, may not be practical for writers. For example, we have the opportunity every day to observe and test out spoken conventions at work. But we may get only one chance to write a statement to the traffic judge. Finally, because most of the situations in which we write are different from one another, the rhetorical conventions for any particular writing situation may be harder to identify. Being an avid reader of fantasy fiction novels may improve your sensitivity to sentence structure and increase your vocabulary, but it is unlikely that such skills will help you understand or apply the conventions of legal correspondence.

Nonetheless, as long as we keep in mind what is unique to the process and medium of writing, the extensive experience we have as speakers who have successfully learned the conventions of the numerous communities through which we move each day provides a useful resource for our development as writers.

Consider some writing situations that might occur in everyday life and how we figure out how to maneuver ourselves in them: a letter of application for a job; instructions for a friend who will be taking care of a pet; or a description of a car accident for the purposes of collecting insurance. We are not likely to have available to study sample letters for the specific job for which we are applying or model instructions for dog sitters. And even if we did, the models would not cover exactly what we needed to say, though they might give us a sense of the tone and phrasing that were acceptable. In these instances, you will probably first draw on what you know about the conventions of spoken language and from there use the lessons of trial and error. You may, for instance, adopt a formal, polite voice in applying for a job, trying to create a respectful, honest image of yourself; for the dog sitter, you may be much more informal and friendly. These general conventions should work for either speech or writing. But at some point, the basic differences between the two ways of communicating will require some differences in the conventions you use.

The most obvious and yet significant difference between spoken and written language is that in the first, both the speaker and the listener are present. In a conversation, we have all the physical cues, gestures, nods of agreement that are not part of written discourse. Having these cues available, hand movements, eye contact, and so on, the speaker can provide a great deal of nonverbal information that the writer cannot. In addition, the listener's response or reaction to the speaker's words can indicate what information is clear or unclear so that the speaker can add details as they are needed by the listener. The presence of a responding listener and, in many cases, a much more open-ended period of time to work in means that it is acceptable for spoken language to be more repetitive and less focused than written language.

Because of this essential difference between speech and writing—the presence of the audience—the conventions of one are not always applicable to the other. Telling the pet sitter in person about your dog—with the dog right there!—you don't necessarily have to remember every detail because the dog's presence will provide a great deal of information and the sitter can immediately ask you for clarification. In a note, it would be problematic to write in a similarly nondetailed way: including no information about the visibly obvious temperament of your dog may result in injury to the pet sitter; forgetting to mention that the dog has just recovered from hip surgery may result in improper care for the dog.

In our other hypothetical situation with an insurance company, the amount of information you provide is also critical. If you are telling the claims adjuster about your car accident, he can stop you when he has heard enough detail on one point, asking you for information on another. However, in writing to the insurance company, if you repeat the story of the car accident several times with slightly different emotional levels, you may unintentionally discredit yourself as a reliable witness.

Because speech provides much more immediate response, we can learn its conventions more easily than we might with writing. In speaking, we receive reaction from our listener to each phrase and word. We can even adjust our conventions along the way, changing "Tom" to "Mr. Kent" when Mr. Kent raises his eyebrows disapprovingly, shortening explanations when Mr. Kent looks impatiently at his watch. While it is true that we can learn some of the conventions of written language in a trial-and-error way similar to the way we learn conventions of speech, the response we receive from a reader to our writing is most often neither as immediate nor as specific as is a listener's response to our speech. This distance between the writer and audience reduces the efficiency with which we rewrite and the opportunity to actually do so. If, for instance, the insurance adjuster to whom you write turns down your claim, it is unlikely that she will point out the specific features of your letter that made your argument unconvincing and ask you for a revision!

Select an essay, written exam, or other piece of writing on which an instructor has written comments. Reread both what you wrote and the instructor's comments. Make a list of any broken conventions that the instructor noted. Although the instructor may not have used the term *conventions*, these kinds of errors would include issues of essay structure or format, use of appropriate terminology, the way information is cited or referenced, or using an expected degree of formality in your choice of words.

Making Your Points

All of the essays you write in *Writing Your Way Through College* require that you find what interests you about a topic, how you feel connected to it, and, from that, develop a focus for writing. A challenge for writers is determining how to hold on to these personal connections, to what sparks their interest in a topic while, at the same time, meeting the requirements of college writing conventions and expectations. That spark—what interests, amuses, concerns, or irritates writers and leads them to their purpose for writing—is what motivates them to write. Yet sometimes, in the course of making adjustments for conventions, writers can lose their enthusiasm for the point they want to make or even lose track of it altogether.

We have claimed several times that writing and speaking are most effective when they grow from something one cares about, is interested in, wants to convey, or wants to make happen. This personal connection is more often apparent in spoken language than in written language. That is, you most often speak because you want to, because you have something to say. Granted, there are times when you feel forced to answer questions or present information. But the majority of the time, and certainly when you were a child first learning to talk, the words came from your own urge to say something. In familiar situations, when the conventions are well known to you, you are able to focus all of your attention on *what* it is you want to say. Sometimes, as you move outside familiar language communities, or in familiar but stressful situations, the complex sets of conventions you encounter can make it more difficult to stay focused on your reason for speaking.

Returning to the earlier scenario of having to tell the mall store manager that there is an error in your bill, you may know, according to convention, that you should talk directly to the store manager, using a respectful, inquiring tone, selecting words that are somewhat formal ("I believe there has been an error" rather than "You are wrong!"). But in the course of keeping these conventions in mind as you speak, what you want to say may be obscured or even lost. Your desire to be polite may become momentarily more important than the fact that you are short on cash and need to have the money refunded right away. Being deferential to the manager's authority may prevent your own knowledge from clearly coming through, and you may appear unsure. This conflict explains why speakers sometimes find themselves speaking inappropriately in stressful settings—we know what the conventions are, that we are to be polite, but we are afraid of losing track of our purpose, so we rush ahead and speak in ways we might not otherwise, shouting at the store manager that he is a fool for making such a mistake. At least we've said what we are thinking, though we have probably lost our chance to be listened to by the manager. It's easy to leave such situations only to realize that we never accomplished what we intended in the first place.

Making Your Points in Writing

As with speech, in writing the difficulty of hanging on to the point we want to make increases as we move farther from familiar language communities. Attaching a note to the TV for your roommate that instructs: "Don't delete the show I recorded last night on TIVO; I haven't watched the last episode!" you have made your point quite clear. Writing a letter to the director of financial aid to inquire about why you have not yet received your funding may be more complicated. In your attempt to follow convention, to sound polite and formal, the seriousness of your request may get lost.

In the absence of a face-to-face audience, writers attempt to address the needs of an imaginary audience, and this makes it easy for writers to become so focused on the conventions that their reason for writing becomes not just overshadowed but completely lost. The conventions can gain an inappropriate advantage. Writers may find themselves adopting an awkward, unnatural use of language that exaggerates conventions and, consequently, the effect of these conventions on the reader. The way we would begin a business meeting in speaking ("Thank you for seeing me") may become exaggerated and uncharacteristically formal in writing ("I am deeply grateful for the opportunity which you have given me to convey the urgency of my concern"). While the second version is not incorrect, it does risk undermining the purpose of the letter—to be heard as a serious student with a valid problem, not as someone who seems uncertain and needs to overstate the situation.

---

26 **Reflection**
Finding Conventions in What You Read

Write about how writing conventions appear in an academic textbook. Underline any phrases, words, or sentence structures in a few pages of a textbook in a course you are taking in your prospective major or any other course in which you are especially interested. Looking over what you have underlined, select three or four that you find most representative and write out your observations about how each convention is intended to help instruct the content of the book.

Creating Your Self with Language

Whenever you write or speak, the words you use and the way you put them together present listeners or readers with an image of who you are. We referred to the writer's self when we discussed the stance a writer takes in relation to his or her reader and the subject of the writing. You can create a formal, distant, general self with phrases like "One can contemplate one's future and life in the next millennium," or an informal, personal, chatty self with "I've got to think about what I'll do after I graduate." This construction of the self, what Aristotle called *ethos*, is the image of the writer created for readers by the writer's word choices and the way he or she puts them together (Cooper 1960). In familiar situations where you speak with confidence, you can, with little thought, easily focus on your purpose and creating an effective ethos. By contrast, in unfamiliar situations, you may be required to give more conscious attention to the image you are projecting.

In spoken language, the speaker's past connection with the listener also contributes to the creation of ethos. For example, imagine the contrast between asking a friend to loan you money and asking a bank. Though you will want to convince both the bank and your friend that you will repay the money, the way you present yourself to each will be different. Your spoken voice is already familiar to your friend and is closely tied to the image of you that your friend already has. The ethos you present in your request to your friend will necessarily either be consistent with the image your friend has of you (a reliable, conscientious person) or attempt to replace your familiar image (an unpredictable con artist) with one that is more reassuring (a person who has seen the error of his ways and wants to be responsible). In contrast, the bank manager has never met you and may have never seen you or heard your voice. You are creating from scratch a spoken self for the bank manager without any past history to rely on or play against.

Finally, in conversation, knowing the conventions and hanging on to your purpose at the risk of hurting the way others think of you may create unexpected or unwanted consequences. For instance, you get someone to cover for you at your job, but your coworkers conclude that you are irresponsible and cannot be relied on. Your sister does your chores, but she tells your parents you are a bully. The store corrects your charges, but the clerks are rude to you every time you come in after this event. Clearly, learning how to speak with authority is more than just learning how to get what you want. Part of getting what you want includes getting people to see you the way you want them to.

As we have mentioned, your spoken self is closely tied to your physical presence and voice. To some listeners, your words may sound differently if you are wearing jeans and a T-shirt than they will if you wear a business suit. In addition, the presence of the listener will affect the way you choose to present yourself. The image you project will be, in part, a response to the person with whom you are speaking. You may decide to present yourself differently as you plan your speech about why you don't deserve a parking ticket depending on whether the judge is a scowling, impatient senior member of the bar or a young, attractive new magistrate.

Unfortunately, both listeners and speakers may let their impressions or biases inappropriately influence the communication taking place. As with any other judgment made from superficial information, these judgments may be a distortion. The scowling magistrate may actually be the more open-minded judge; the speaker dressed in jeans may be the more formidable. In focusing on appearances, we may miscalculate how we should present ourselves. We may find ourselves speaking overly formally to the older judge and too casually to the younger.

Creating a Written Self

When we write, these difficulties of creating one's identity are magnified since we can only imagine our audience. With no immediate presence of a reader, writers may, initially, rely too much on the dictates of convention to create a written self. For example, the conventions of business letter writing may require formality, but the purpose of your letter, to get the attention of the financial aid office, may be severely weakened if these conventions conflict with the points you wish to make. To ensure that the written self you create is consistent with your purpose for writing, you need to create an appropriate image of the reader. When you write to a stranger or a near stranger, it may be especially challenging to adjust your writing to this imagined audience. Writing to the director of financial aid, you may be intimidated by the image you have created, an image that may be far more imposing than would be the actual human presence, so your writing can become defensive even though you have not been directly challenged. You may have invented an unfriendly, narrow-minded man who cares more about protecting the university's money than about your need to pay your bills:

> Dear Sir:
> You must think that students can survive without the funds that were promised them and that we are just taking the university's money because we are lazy slackers.

Creating, instead, the image of a director who knows that students depend on financial support and sees his job as that of helping students, you may adjust your written self to one that is more agreeable:

Dear Sir:

I recognize that the financial aid office must keep track of the needs of hundreds of students at once. Unfortunately, my funding did not arrive when I was told it would last week, so I hope you can investigate my case as soon as possible. As you know, like most students receiving financial support, I cannot stay in school without these funds.

Writing provides us with an opportunity to examine the images we hold of our audience and to create a sense of audience that serves us best as communicators.

---

27 Reflection
Identifying Your Written Self

Analyze the written self created in the piece of writing whose response you considered in Reflection 25. Write about the ethos your writing creates and how it does so. What seems to have been the image of the audience that you had in mind and how was your ethos created in relation to that audience? Identify and list particular words or sentences in the piece that create these images of you and of the audience.

How Changing Media Affect Your Written Self

Aside from the purpose and audience for which you are writing, one other feature powerfully influences the self you create when you write: the medium in which you are writing. Even if the purpose is the same, the medium you use will result in differences not only in the way you write but also in the content of the writing and in the words and structures you use. Moreover, the medium itself becomes a convention, a choice that may or may not be appropriate in a given situation. We can easily imagine the physical differences and improved ease of writing as the ink bottle and quill were replaced by the ink cartridge pen or when the typewriter became outmoded by the word processor. But beyond making the physical act of writing and revising easier, the media of the twenty-first century are also closely tied to conventions of writing and the creation of the writer's self. Convention determines, in part, whether we communicate via a paper letter or the Internet. And once that choice is made, there are conventions regarding which component of the Internet (email, instant message, list server, chatroom, blog, social networking websites like

Facebook and Myspace, and so on) and the encodedness of the language we choose to use. For example, after a job interview, it is conventional in business to write a thank-you note to the head interviewer, but is this to be a letter on paper, an email message, or a text message? While most of us would argue for either the first or the second choice, the way you write the message must either overcome the inherent informality of email or assume that your audience finds such informality appropriate. The speed with which a message arrives, the apparent carefulness of its creation, and its perceived degree of privacy all contribute to the medium's impact.

New media also include the use of nontext material, photos, drawings, graphics, as well as hyperlinks to video and sound clips. And so, in addition to creating ethos by means of the words you select, you begin the process of creating ethos with the very medium you select.

---

28 Reflection
Conventions in Technology

Identify and write about the conventions of nonprint communication directed to different audiences. Although no one ever taught you the conventions of email or instant or text messaging, you are probably quite familiar with them. Look closely at some IMs, emails, text messages, or Facebook or Myspace comments you have written to different audiences and explain what some of these conventions are (acceptable topics, abbreviations, emoticons, codes, etc.), how you came to learn them, and how they vary among audiences.

CHAPTER
7

Interacting with Written Texts

Reading and Writing for Essays 5 and 6

The Nature of College Writing

Writing textbooks, including this one, create an illusion about the way we learn to write and become better writers. The illusion is that once you have read this book, completed its assignments, and written all of the essays, you will be done becoming a college writer; you will have finished the book and the course, and will have learned all you need to know about writing. We certainly believe that when you have finished this textbook and the writing for this course, you will be a better, more self-confident writer. But you won't be done becoming a writer. For, as we have suggested throughout *Writing Your Way Through College*, you will always have new choices to make as a writer; new situations to write in; new ideas to communicate; and new audiences to write for. Until this point, we have focused on the broad community of college writing, but as you will, or have already, found out, this large community is divided into the smaller communities of academic departments and disciplines. During your years as a student, you will frequently find yourself in new contexts, writing for the demands of different disciplines with varying conventions and expectations.

Of course, if there were no consistencies in college writing experiences, college writing texts would not be possible. Throughout this book, we have identified some of the conventions that remain relatively constant for all college writing. Academic readers have expectations about the directness with which you need to express the points you make, the authority you establish as a writer, the need for explicit analysis and elaboration of ideas, the appropriateness of information sources, the clarity with which you identify these sources, and the use of standardized English. They have expectations about what counts as evidence and what counts as *convincing* evidence. Necessarily, the expectations of academic readers like your instructors influence the choices that college writers make as they learn how to use appropriate conventions, focus a college essay, provide evidence for the points of the essay, and create a compelling ethos or image of themselves for the reader.

Writing with a Formula

Because writing is by nature so time-consuming, most students wish for a formula that would make writing quicker and easier, a generic program the writer could plug ideas into, push the Print button, and come up with a perfect essay every time. Although, as we will explain later, for almost all college writing assignments you will need to figure out what matters in that setting to that instructor, for some very particular writing occasions, you can make use of a formatting formula. In fact, there are conventions that are so rigid and expected that they do become very much like a formula. And when there is a formula of sorts, there is also a reason the formula exists, one that has to do with the general purpose of the piece of writing.

First, you may have already come across some disciplines for which formula-type writing is more expected than others. In business memos or scientific lab reports there are often quite rigid formats that writers are expected to follow. In these instances, the point of the writing is to convey information as quickly and directly as possible. Keep in mind, though, that these are *formats* within which information is to be presented. Even in formula writing, writers still have the job of coming up with ideas, conveying their message, appropriately addressing the audience, and so on.

A second and most familiar example of college writing that has a formula is the timed writing exam. Students receive a question and are asked to write on the spot for a given time period. Writers of timed exams are not expected to develop ideas and find meanings to the extent that they are expected to do so in untimed writing. Exams are an occasion to present quickly what you already know on a given question. Unless another pattern for the formula is given, you can usually rely on the following:

1. a brief introduction that restates the question or provides some background
2. a brief statement of one or two highly explicit points you wish to make

3. several paragraphs or pages of specific explanation of these points using supporting examples
4. some brief concluding statements that reflect on the question and the information you have provided

Readers of a timed essay do not usually expect to learn something new, as would the reader of an untimed essay. They expect to be able quickly to see if you have learned certain concepts or principles or remembered certain information.

This same formula is also expected in timed essay exams that are not connected to specific course material, such as writing placement or exit exams. You may be given some reading material or a question to respond to. Again, readers of these exams are not looking for your unique perspective or your creative process in the way they might be were you writing an untimed essay. The formula listed above will be useful to you on these occasions as well.

Learning the Conventions of College Writing

Aside from the very particular college writing situation we have just described, to be successful in most others, you will have to determine what matters to a certain academic reader and why. Because this opens up such a broad spectrum of options—seemingly as broad as the number of instructors and courses in college—the conventions of college writing may seem to be a mysterious code known only to instructors and not to be broken by students. Yet these conventions can be learned in the same way we learn those for all language: by trial and error, by observation, and by direct instruction. Unfortunately, like many writers in new situations, writers new to college may rely on the least efficient of these ways of learning conventions: trial and error.

Trial and error is particularly ineffective as a means of learning college writing conventions because the feedback students receive to their writing in the form of general comments or grades does not usually provide enough of the kind of information writers need in order to improve their writing. You may have experienced the frustration of trying to figure out how to keep the quality of your writing the same or how to improve it when the only prior information you have from an instructor is a broad category label such as an A or a C.

Since each academic discipline at the university—history, biology, English, psychology, mathematics, and so forth—is a unique area of focus with its own significant questions and ways of examining its subject, college writing conventions are especially complex. That is, the grades and comments from an instructor in one discipline or subject area may not be applicable when you write in another discipline. Some of the qualities that your biology instructor liked about your writing may not be valued in an essay you write for history. Rather than relying on trial and error, college writers can benefit from careful observation in a course or among courses within a department in order to learn the conventions and expectations for an individual discipline.

To appreciate the complexity of college writing conventions, consider, for example, that although several disciplines on campus may have courses available on the topic of man-made disasters, the conventions for examining and writing about the topic will vary dramatically among the departments. In the English department, you might read a novel like Carolyn See's *Golden Days* and write a feminist analysis of the main character; in the political science department you might outline and examine the political events leading up to Hiroshima and Nagasaki, writing an argument for or against U.S. action; in environmental studies you might visit the decontaminated site of a nuclear waste dump, interviewing local residents about the effects on their neighborhood; and in the journalism department you might recollect and analyze your own investigation and interviews related to nuclear disarmament or waste, writing a profile piece of your retrospective account. So while the starting point, man-made disaster, is the same, in each course, the object and perspective of study, the kind of information that is collected and valued (personal experience, observation and interviews, or written texts), and the focus of the writing are quite different.

As a college writer, what you are learning through observation of the people and materials in a particular discipline are the ways professionals in that discipline think and write; what questions they find significant; what sources of information and methods of analysis they most value. Although the general college writing conventions we listed at the start of this chapter will hold for all disciplines, unique disciplinary conventions need to be acquired as you move through various courses.

To begin determining what are the appropriate conventions for a discipline, carefully observe the content and materials of a course or a series of courses in a department. Here are some questions that might guide your observations:

1. What kinds of information are most frequently cited in the readings for a particular course?

2. What kinds of sources does the instructor most often introduce in lecture and discussion?

3. Look closely at the assignments. What kinds of questions seem to recur—those about history? Personal experience? Other people? Specific readings?

4. Look at the course syllabus. What does the instructor seem to value and how will your performance in the course be measured?

5. Look at the required texts. What is the tone of voice that is used by the authors—what is the ethos that is created? How is it created?

6. If sample essays have been distributed, how are the writers making and supporting the points they make? What is the ethos that is projected?

7. Read carefully any comments the instructor has made on your writing. What conventions does he or she seem to be valuing most?

Reflection
Figuring Out What Counts in a Course

Using the materials from a class you are taking (other than this one) or a class you have recently taken, answer the questions in the preceding list. You might choose a course in the department you may be selecting as your major or a course you especially liked. These materials can include the syllabus, course assignments, essay assignments, and the instructor's comments and corrections. Analyze them to determine what seems to matter to that instructor in that particular course and, by extension, to the related discipline. Be sure to identify and write down what you found in the course materials that led you to your conclusions. Finally, record some general observations you can make about writing and writing conventions in that class.

Besides using these kinds of observations to understand academic conventions and expectations, the third way for college writers to learn conventions is direct instruction from or discussion with a teacher. By talking to an instructor, you can move beyond the course conventions to find out about the written conventions of the academic discipline within which the course is located.

Reflection
Interviewing an Instructor

Arrange to meet with and interview or contact by email an instructor who teaches the class you examined in the previous reflection. This can be the instructor you had or a different instructor. Use the following questions (and others of your own design if you wish) to find out from the instructor about the conventions of the discipline within which that course is taught. Let the instructor know that you are collecting this information for a writing class or for future writing assignments you will complete in the course. Be sure to bring the list of questions with you to your meeting. Take careful notes on what the instructor tells you.

1. What are the major journals and books in the discipline?
2. To what national professional organizations does the instructor belong or is the discipline affiliated?
3. What kinds of writing are most often done in this discipline?
4. How are the essays or reports structured?
5. What manner of citation is used?
6. What kind of research is most valued?
7. Where are the most convincing materials likely to be published?

Multiple Sets of Conventions

Over years of teaching, most instructors develop their own unique sets of writing conventions—features of writing that are particular to the expectations in their classes and assignments. These might take the form of a particular layout for a cover page or a way of annotating a bibliography. In addition to these personalized conventions are those that are dictated by the discipline within which the instructor works. That is, the instructor holds you responsible for the particular conventions that he or she has developed over years of teaching, and, at the same time, the discipline you are working in has its own additional (sometimes complementary, sometimes contradictory) conventions. So, for instance, your Biology 101 instructor makes a lab assignment that is defined both by his own set of conventions or rules for writing and also by those of the discipline of biology. And while, for the most part, these sets of conventions are consistent with one another, when you take your next-level biology course, from a different instructor, you will find out which conventions were unique to the first instructor and which are consistent throughout and dictated by the discipline. Another way to determine which conventions are particular to the discipline and which to an individual instructor is to look at the published texts in the discipline to see what features they share, what consistencies in style, formatting, voice, data sources, and so on, you see across journals.

31   **Reflection**
Conventions of Journals in an Academic Discipline

Find several journals from the lists you created in the two previous reflections. You may collect these either from the library or from the Internet. Look through the journals for the most obvious visual conventions: How long do the articles tend to be? What is the nature of article titles? What kinds of citations are used? Are articles written by one author or by two or more authors? Are there headings, charts, and graphics? Make a list of what you find.

Making Your Point

As you continue to grow and develop as a college writer, you may find that the very conventions and expectations that we have been describing and that you are working so hard to understand and employ seem to frustrate, even prevent, your attempts to make a particular point in your essays. Student writers can become so focused on the formula, on figuring out what the teacher wants, that they can find themselves unable to locate what they, themselves want to say. Remember that one of the central identifying features of college writing is that it makes its meaning explicit. This can occur only if writers know what that meaning is—what they feel the urge to argue, explain, describe, propose—and, equally important, why they want to share that meaning.

Language, both spoken and written, most often emerges from the speaker's or writer's urge to say something to an audience. But because college writing is initiated by someone else, by an instructor, students are faced with a difficult dilemma: If the writing is initiated by someone else and must adhere to externally imposed conventions, how can you find within these constraints your own urge to write? And how, while paying attention to the conventions, can you hang on to your own purposes?

Your personal and cultural perspectives offer valuable connections to the writing you will do in college. One of our goals in designing the reflections and the essay assignments in *Writing Your Way Through College* is for you to try out writing strategies that draw from these perspectives and give you a way to find your own urge for writing within assigned writing prompts. A second, connected goal is to help you learn how to convey your own purposes for writing within the parameters of the conventions set by the instructor and the discipline. To write effectively in college, you need to ask yourself; What do I have to say and how can I say it in such a way that I will be listened to?

---

32 **Reflection**
Conveying Your Reason to Write Within the Conventions of the Discipline

Write about an essay or piece of assigned writing that you completed in the course whose materials you examined in Reflection 29. Identify the purpose you had for writing. What conventions of that discipline did you use to make your purpose clear to a reader?

Creating a Written Self

As a college writer, you have choices about the written self, or ethos, you will create with your words for the reader of your text. But like the choices you have about using conventions and making your points, choices about ethos in college writing come with their own peculiar challenges.

The majority of college essays are written at the request of an instructor who will be the primary, though often not the only, reader or audience. In relation to you, the student writer, this audience has more education, has studied the subject of the essay enough to have become a specialist in that particular discipline, and holds the power of evaluation and grading. Faced with such an audience, sometimes students choose to meet the instructor head-on, attempting to create an image that will impress the reader with its intelligence. However, while seeking to develop an impressive, intelligent voice or self-image, students can mistake wording for convention. That is, they act on an assumption that college writing is defined simply by its language, by the inclusion of big, formal vocabulary and complicated sentences. What the student overlooks in this approach is the reason that particular vocabulary and syntax are used and their relationship to the conventions and expectations of the discipline.

For example, trying to sound academic when writing about a novel, one student might write, "Everything about the characters is discerned as the story progresses." Writing about the same idea, a more experienced college writer might instead write, "The narrator maintains an omniscient perspective throughout the novel." Both writers are making an observation about the amount of information that is shared in the story.

The second student knows, and chooses to use, some of the specialized language characteristic of literary writing. Using words like *narrator, omniscient,* and *novel,* the writer can be identified as someone familiar with the conventionally accepted language of literature. Instead of selecting familiar vocabulary and syntax or using specialized language that is appropriate to the discipline, the first writer used thesaurus speak, substituting *discerned* for *known,* and created an unnatural sentence construction with no active subject (no one is doing the discerning). In an attempt to create an academic, impressive voice, students can inadvertently mark themselves as being unfamiliar with the discipline by using uncommon, uncomfortable language. In fact, the most experienced college writers might not try to rely on individual words pulled from a thesaurus or a literary glossary at all. Instead, these writers would know that what matters most to the literary college reader is that an essay has a concrete observation followed by support drawn from the text itself.

The third student uses the most conventional version of the idea cast in the two other sentences by writing, "In *The Great Gatsby,* Nick speaks as if he knows everything about every other character."

Think back to our earlier example of the operating room. What would happen if someone who was not a medical person and had only a patient's knowledge of health care tried to use medical terminology in the same way the doctors were? Instead of conveying the voice of a knowledgeable physician or someone on par with the doctors, this person would be marked as an outsider who was pretending badly. The same thing can happen in college writing if one tries to create a voice for the purpose of impressing a reader by using words or sentence structures that are unfamiliar.

It is as if you are going out with friends and decide, at the last minute, that your jacket is too ordinary, but it's the only one you have. You run to the closet and grab your brother's new leather jacket, which is several sizes too large for you. When your friends see you, they notice the jacket all right, but what they notice is that it doesn't fit.

There is little chance that you can sound like one of your instructors or that you can successfully create an image similar to a professor's. Indeed, as a college student, that is not what is expected of you by your instructors. Through the kind of close observation and instruction we have described, you can develop a sense of the special (not necessarily big) vocabulary that your instructor uses and that appears in the texts you read in class. You can also come to understand what kind of information counts in that course and how it is expected to be presented. Finally, you can take advantage of the perspective you have by way of your own personal and cultural experiences, letting these provide you with insight into whatever you are writing.

In this way, the image you create of yourself and the voice you use will be appropriate to what you want to say, appropriate to the conventions of the discipline, and consistent with your relationship to those conventions. You will provide readers with the image of a writer worth listening to, a writer who brings a certain authority to the text, and who presents himself or herself in a manner respectful of the conventions of the conversation he or she is entering.

---

33   Reflection
Creating a Written Self

Return to the paper you considered in the previous reflection to determine what kind of voice you created in this writing. Make a list of words or language structures that allowed you to create this voice. Describe, too, how this voice is appropriate to the discipline in which you were writing. Where else have you heard this voice in the writing or speech of the discipline?

Valuing and Evaluating Written Academic Texts

As we have suggested, one final feature that distinguishes college writing from most other kinds of writing and that adds to its level of difficulty is that it often requires the writer to interact with published texts. While writers outside the university *may* draw on what they have read to inform their writing, inside the university it is *essential* for writers to know what has been said, in print, about their subjects. And the more academic a piece of writing is, the more heavily referenced it will be. A doctoral dissertation, for example, usually includes a full chapter or two entirely devoted to what has been said so far on the subject under investigation, quoting from these texts and establishing the groundwork for the original material the dissertation will explore. If that same study were to be rewritten for a nonacademic audience, it would likely make much less extensive reference to the background material and would document its sources less prominently in the text.

All academic writing requires evidence to support the points a writer makes. Writers must consider, in relation to the subject of their writing, the value and reliability of each available information source: observing and listening, one's own recollections and memories, and written texts. That is, if you want to find out about teens' use of slang by observing and listening, you might go to a teen who uses slang or maybe a high school teacher who hears such slang, but you probably would not ask a resident of a retirement community whose only encounter with teens is his one grandson. Similarly, if your source of information is your recollected experiences, you would include those that you can recall in the greatest detail and clarity and that seem most relevant to the subject that is the focus of your essay.

Like these sources of information, the material you will gather from the third source of information, written texts, is not all of equal value, nor can it all be cited with equal authority. To some degree, words that appear in print or across the lines of an electronic computerized network give the illusion of being important, so evaluating sources becomes even more significant.

Depending on the academic discipline in which you are writing, different texts will have greater influence and credibility. Written texts can include academic and general-audience books, essays and articles from professional journals, newspaper and magazine articles, reference materials, or government documents. These materials can appear in print form or on the Internet. Some electronic sources replicate those we can find in the library: articles, newspapers, conference papers, journals, and so forth; others have been created specifically for electronic rather than print distribution, such as webpages, online databases, online journals, online magazines, and so on.

Because anyone who has access to the technology and knows how to make use of it can create a webpage or an electronic database, and because many of the tens of thousands of books and articles published each year are done so with little or no evaluation of their quality or reliability, writers must determine which written texts will provide their essays with the best, most credible means of support.

Primary and Secondary Sources

Most academic fields make a distinction between primary and secondary sources. Primary sources are what is studied, and secondary sources are what is written about what has been studied. So, a historian examines some documents and then writes about her analysis of these documents. The documents are the primary source and the essay the historian writes is a secondary source for other historians to read and use in their own research. Some primary sources are print texts such as historical documents, pieces of literature, published interviews, scientific data, and so on. And some primary sources are texts that are not represented in words but are, nonetheless, read by scholars in various fields. This sort of text would include *visual texts* like artwork, image-based advertising, and events of nature; *auditory texts* like music and conversations; *lived-experience texts* such as memories and self-observation; and *social texts* like communities and institutions.

Based on these distinctions, we include as the primary sources for essay assignments 1 and 2 the auditory texts of what people say; for Essays 3 and 4 the sources are the text of lived experience and your own memories; and for Essays 5 and 6 the sources are written academic texts. In each case, you will be expected to create the secondary text, an essay that reflects on and analyzes these primary sources.

This process of analyzing some text in order to produce your own text may be said to be the essential work of the academy. The vast scholarship in all academic fields depends not only on the study of primary sources but also on the study of secondary material. Specialists in any area must keep up with what is going on in their field, and they do this by reading each other's work.

Using Academic Texts as Primary Sources

To use academic texts effectively, you need to know that they are reliable sources. When you have personal knowledge about the people from whom you collect information, you know they can be relied on for certain kinds of information but not for others; similarly, you know personally the extent to which the details of your recollections and memories are reliable. However, when you select and use written texts to inform your thinking, you must rely on others' determinations of their credibility.

In the academic world, this determination is based, among other things, on the authority and reputation of the authors and the means by which the texts were made public. Generally speaking, texts that have been written by individuals who are known to have particular expertise in an area and texts that have been published through organizations (publishers, editorial boards, review boards, and so forth) that screen and evaluate for quality and truth value provide the most valuable and convincing data for college writers.

For example, recall what you learned from the instructor you interviewed in a previous reflection about the journals in his or her discipline. Only a few journals are most read and respected in any discipline. Many more essays than those published are submitted to the journal's editor, a person who has, by virtue of being editor, already reached a certain status level. In the most authoritative and trusted journals, the procedures for selecting essays are also the most professional: essays are read by two or more reviewers, who must come to agreement about whether or not an essay is up-to-date, interesting, and well written enough to be published. Once selected, an essay is then put through a fact check, where another set of readers determines whether the information and citations are factual and accurate. Readers expect that by the time the journals reach them, the essays have survived a gauntlet of checks and counterchecks. This is not to say that journals not on this select list are dishonest or without value. But it does mean that readers need to look closely at the front pages of the journal, where its selection procedures are described, or to confirm that the essays in the journal are authored by individuals whose own reputations provide a high degree of reliability.

Electronic texts, as well, need to be evaluated in these terms. Since professional and scholarly organizations make use of the Web, academic texts are often distributed there. But a vast amount of what is on the Web is self-published or published by groups or organizations with no credibility in the academic world. So, while the web provides an indispensable resource for college writers, the material published there needs to be evaluated carefully for its value and credibility. One initial indicator of the credibility of any particular Web address is its extension, the last three letters in the address. For academics, the most trustworthy options are *.edu* and *.gov*—the first indicates that the site is sponsored by an educational institution; the second refers to a government-sponsored site. These extensions provide minimal assurance that the site you are visiting has a certain degree of reliability as opposed to those with the final extensions *.net*, *.com*, and *.org*, which can be created by anyone who knows the language of HTML. However, even this distinction can be misleading: some of the most reliable academic sites have a *.org* address, and some *.edu* sites are sponsored by unaccredited schools or those affiliated with extremist philosophies that would not have credibility at most universities.

The most effective way to determine the reliability of any site is by investigating it as you would any publication. Read the information on the site carefully—who is its author and what are his or her qualifications? Is there an "About This Site" link? When was the site published? What kinds of citations or bibliography does the site itself offer? When you put the author's or organization's name into a search engine, what do you learn?

While it may seem to be terribly time-consuming to ask all these questions of the sites you visit or the texts you read, we assure you that it is time well spent. Indeed, this is part of what it means to write in the academic world. One false citation or bogus reference can destroy the integrity of your whole paper. And later on, in your professional life, one such error could potentially cost you your career.

More immediately significant to you, however, is that your paper becomes more credible and your points more valid as you add academic support.

---

34 Reflection
Investigating Websites

List three websites related to the discipline or course you have been investigating in the last several reflections. What do you know about the reliability and authority of each of these sites and how can you be sure of this evaluation?

CHAPTER
8

Essay 1: Learning About Language by Observing and Listening

Composing, Rereading, and Refocusing

Earlier, we described composing, how writers shuttle back and forth between their sense of what they want to say and the words they are selecting. As writers compose, the words they choose help them to generate more words. After we produce some writing, we then reread what we have written. Our rereading reminds us of both what we have already said and what we still want to say. So, in response to what we have written, we write more.

The writing activity of freewriting that you were introduced to earlier helps writers to compose and generate writing. The success of freewriting depends, in part, on not pausing to reread until you get some of your thoughts onto the page and, in that way, not disrupting your concentration as you are coming up with ideas. When you first tried freewriting, it may have been frustrating not to glance back and reread as you usually do when writing. You may have had consciously to resist the urge to stop and reread as you wrote. As you become accustomed to freewriting, you will become more comfortable with this process of quickly generating material—and only then, rereading it. In fact, by postponing the act of reading until it can be given concentrated effort, you will be awarding it the significance it deserves as part of the larger writing process.

Just as expansive freewriting can help you to get your initial thoughts onto the page, effective rereading of what you have written can help you to write even more.

When you actively engage in the process of reading, paying attention to the meaning and to *what* you have written, rather than to *how* you have written it (there will be plenty of time for that later), your reading helps you generate more writing. You can reread with an eye to what more you have to say, to what direction your writing seems to be going, to what questions your writing seems to raise, and so on.

Writing Essays

All of the essay assignments in *Writing Your Way Through College* lead you to write academic college essays. Although you might integrate some creative qualities in your essays—for example, narrative segments, illustrative metaphors, or the creation of a characteristic voice—academic essays are distinct from creative writing in that they make *specific points* for the purpose of conveying *explicit meaning* to a reader. Whereas a story, poem, or play may evoke multiple interpretations for readers, leaving readers to draw their own conclusions, college essays convey explicit meaning. Further, college essays are *analytical*; they examine specific evidence and convey to the reader specific points about the material that the writer is analyzing. There are two aspects to each of the six essay assignments in this text:

1. the subject or question about which you will write
2. the evidence you will gather and analyze to form the focus of your essay

Each essay will evolve from writing that you generate over the course of several chapters. This current chapter, like all the other chapters in which essays are assigned, will present you with a writing assignment and then guide you through a series of exploratory writing activities that will help you gather and analyze your information, focus your interpretations, and move your writing from an initial exploration to a completed essay. Here is a summary of the kinds of activities you can expect:

- analyzing your reflections from various perspectives
- reflecting on what you have written so far or what is still on your mind
- sorting and prioritizing your ideas and questions
- finding a focus for your essay and finding what points you wish to make
- examining the information that you have so far and determining what information you still need to collect

As you create this collection of exploratory writings, you will be moving from initially random thoughts on paper toward writing that is more specific and intentional. If you allow your ideas and your essay to develop in this way, giving yourself space and time to explore and expand ideas early on, you can build a foundation for making a final version of the essay that will be interesting, purposeful, and complete.

In the course of composing drafts of the essays, you will be referred to essays that several of our own students have written in response to these same assignments (in Chapter 14). To help you consider the decisions that these writers made in relation to your own, we have inserted questions and observations into the essays. We have also included guidelines for reading and responding to writers' drafts (in Chapter 15) to provide guidance for getting feedback about your draft as you continue writing and revising. Finally, "Guidelines for Editing Final Revisions" (Chapter 16) will help you to view the language and presentation of your essay in terms of your readers' expectations.

Composing Essay 1: Learning About Language Communities by Observing and Listening

The assignment for Essay 1 appears on page 73. To write this essay, you will need to select some issue or idea related to the general topic of language that you find interesting enough to reflect on it further. That is, although the general subject matter for your essay is language, the specific topic or question you choose is up to you. The notes in your reflections, which provide an initial source for a topic or question, address a variety of concerns: how individuals have been affected by language or have changed their language for different people and settings; how others have or have not been successful at establishing authority in various language settings; the impact of conflicting expectations about the way words and conventions are used when people move from their close-to-home communication communities to school or business or professional communities; the code words or conventions that are used in different situations and what their effect is on different speakers, and so forth.

Once you have completed some exploratory writing and begun to determine a focus for your essay, you will identify the evidence you already have to support and develop your focus as well as what data you still need for additional evidence. For Essay 1 and Essay 2, this data will come primarily from information you collect by observing and listening to other people.

Gathering Data by Observing and Listening

Writers who use conversations and observations—like those recorded in your reflections in Chapters 1 through 3—as a primary source of information are engaging in *field research*, gathering information or data from direct interaction and contact with other people. It is by closely listening to and observing individuals or systematically interviewing them that many anthropologists, psychologists, sociologists, and other social scientists begin their own research. Carefully analyzing their notes, interpreting patterns of response or behavior, these researchers develop theories about particular individuals or about human behavior in general. Frequently, they will return to the field to add to their existing bank of information, seeking additional material for their questions or support for their theories. Similarly, though you already conducted some field research in the course of completing the reflections in the first three chapters of the book, once you have identified a topic or question and begun to determine the focus your essay may take, you will need to collect more information. Besides direct conversation or interviews, you can also gather data from phone or Internet conversation. You can gather information online by sending and receiving emails, logging on to a chatroom conversation, or subscribing to various newsgroups, list servers, and so on. Some of this Internet conversation can be a rich source of information for your field research. Your decisions about whether to use observation, casual conversation or interviews, telephone conversation or email, or various combinations will depend on the focus of your essay and on the kind of information you need to collect.

Evaluating the Information You Collect

Whatever media you use for gathering data, in order to provide adequate and convincing support for the focus of your essay, you will need to evaluate the information you have available and decide whether you need to collect additional or more persuasive references and illustrations. Once you have determined the focus of your essay, you will notice that not all conversations and observations are of equal value or allow you to write with the same authority. For example, if your essay were to focus on the connection between middle school slang and contemporary rap music, it would be more convincing to the reader if the essay included actual examples of slang you overheard at a middle school than it would if you were merely to ask your twelve-year-old sister what slang she uses. Or if you intended to explain the use of coded language in a particular profession, you would not be able to write a convincing illustration had you never spoken with anyone who actually practiced this profession.

Another consideration when you evaluate your information is the authority of any individual source. If, for instance, you enter a general chatroom on the Internet to ask what the other participants think of bilingual education, the information you gather from the resulting conversations will be extremely limited in value by the fact that the speakers have no verifiable knowledge of or experience with the subject. Furthermore, the speakers are anonymous and aren't in any way accountable for what they say. However, were you to join a newsgroup or list server designed for elementary school teachers, the views of the speakers, who would identify themselves by name and school affiliation, would carry considerable authority.

35   Reflection
Learning from Students' Drafts

Sometime during the process of drafting your essay, turn to the student essays in Chapter 14. In particular, look at the essays in which writers used information gathered by listening to and observing others. In each of these essays, writers selected places or people about whom they were curious or wanted to learn more and took careful notes about what they saw and heard, about what the people they interviewed said. Then, using these notes as a place to begin their analysis, the writers found a focus for their writing, something they wanted to say and that they could develop and support with the information they had collected.

Read these essays, noticing how these writers made clear the focus of their essays and used information to support their points. Then answer the questions that we have embedded in each essay.

Exploratory Writing Activities for Creating Your Essay

The following exploratory writing activities are intended to help you examine your ideas, generate and develop new ones, gather more information as your ideas grow, and, ultimately, draft an essay. As you will see, because these activities include lots of writing and encourage you to collect and evaluate more information, they cannot be done in one sitting, but over the course of several hours or several days. However your instructor paces you through this writing, we recommend that you begin by scanning all of the activities to get a sense of where you are headed.

1. Questions and Connections

Reread the reflections that you completed in the first three chapters. Look for ways that you can make connections among them. Jot down these connections. You might consider questions such as What do your reflections illustrate about how people acquire the privilege or authority to speak in different situations? What do they suggest about how the conventions of language seem to shift across situations? Do any of the ways in which language is used or authority is awarded seem to compete with one another? Looking at those reflections in which you exchanged stories or information with another writer, did you find that your experiences were similar or not? What conclusions can you draw from these observations? What is there in any of the individual reflections that seems particularly intriguing to you? Are there some about which you have more to say? What questions do any of the reflections raise for you?

2. Conflicting Points of View

Create a dialogue between speakers of two different language communities. Try out different possible scenarios. Remember that language communities can include those of specific hobbies, professions, interest groups, as well as neighborhoods, regions, and ethnic groups.

Write a second dialogue that evolves differently than the first. Then, reread what you have written and write your reflections on these language communities.

3. Metaphoric Thinking

Writers often explore a concept by making a comparison between it and something else. Metaphoric thinking allows writers to look at their thoughts in a fresh and sometimes unexpected way.

Identify a concept or issue that appears in or is suggested by the writing you have done so far, and write out two or three comparisons between the original concept and something else that seems appropriate. (For example, talking to my boss is like . . . ; my friend's story about her family is like . . . ; the language of politics is like . . . ; and so on.) Next, explain these comparisons. Write for a few minutes about how a comparison works, looking for what the comparison shows you about the concept that you might not have otherwise noticed.

4. Listing Ideas That Interest You

Reread the first three exploratory activities. Quickly list subjects that interest you so far by asking yourself what questions and issues your thinking about language and language communities has raised. What bothers you or interests you? What would you most like to know more about? This list provides a quick snapshot of some of what is going on in your mind in relation to the assignment at this time.

5. Selecting the Ideas Most Interesting to You

Underline two items from your list that currently look most inviting. Write briefly—five to ten minutes—about each one. You can make your initial decisions on any basis you choose, narrowing down to the two items on the list that seem to be the most compelling subjects, ones you would not mind giving a few minutes of your attention to today. The writing you do about each idea is expected to be unfocused and is intended to explore your knowledge, feelings, state of mind about each item.

When you are finished writing, reread these two brief writings and select the one about which you have the most to say, the most curiosity, the greatest feeling, or even the greatest confusion.

6. Identifying an Emerging Focus for Your Essay

Skim through all of the pages you have written in these activities, paying special attention to the writing you completed for activity 5 about a particular subject for your essay. Now, determine what explicit focus your first draft will have in relation to this subject. Expect this focus to shift and evolve as you write and collect more data. At this moment, before starting a first draft, what focus do you anticipate that it will have? What particular meaning do you want to convey with your essay?

Once you have written a couple of sentences that identify what this focus will be, look at the data or information you have gathered. What in the data you have collected will be useful to you for this focus? What does the data tell you or what do you want to use the data to say?

7. Reflecting on the Information

a. *What do you already know?* Thinking about the topic or question you have chosen, freewrite on what you already know about this topic. Describe what you know in detail. Tell about your current feelings and understanding.

b. *What do you need to know?* Write about what more you need to find out. What questions do you have? What do you want to know?

c. *How can you find out more?* Write down ways that you might find answers to the questions you listed in the previous step. Can you find out more about your topic by listening to people talk or by observing? What will you be looking for as you observe? What kinds of questions might you ask other people?

d. *What can you never know?* Write down the kinds of things that you could never understand about the topic. What is it that would prevent that understanding?

8. Gathering More Information

Considering the focus of your essay and reviewing the writing you have done so far, what more information do you need? What additional field research should you do? There may be a place you need to visit again or additional people with whom you need to speak. As you draft and revise you can always pause at other points, as well, to collect whatever seems to be missing. In order to make the process of gathering information most useful and productive, plan carefully the questions you will ask, the conversations you need to hear, which stories and recollections you need to be retold.

Allow at least a few days to conduct this research, being sure to take complete and specific notes about what you hear or are told and the identity of the speakers.

9. Visual Thinking

As a final activity before starting your first draft try an activity recommended by one of our students, Michael Wright. Make a brief sketch, diagram, or design in which you remind yourself of what is, so far, the focus of your essay. Then, in whatever visual format works for you, arrange the information or data you have selected to help you make your points convincing and supportive of your focus.

Writing a First Draft of Your Essay

Using the focus that you identified earlier and drawing on the information or data that you have gathered, write a first draft of an essay in which you make your initial attempt to present and support the particular meaning you want to convey to your readers.

Because this is a college essay, by the time you finish revising your drafts, the point of the essay should be explicitly clear to the reader and the information you have gathered should develop or support that point. However, because this is an early draft, don't worry too much yet about the correctness or completeness of what you are writing. There will be time for you to change sentences, rearrange ideas, and add or delete information later.

Once your draft is complete, you and your classmates can use the guidelines in Chapters 15 and 16 to revise and edit your draft as you move toward completing the final revision for your instructor.

CHAPTER
9

Essay 2: Learning About a Subject of Your Choice by Observing and Listening

Reconsidering the Process of Writing

For the first essay assignment, we identified the general subject matter of language and language communities. From within that broad subject, you had the challenges of selecting a particular topic or question on which you wanted to reflect and of collecting appropriate information or evidence by talking and listening to others. The focus of your essay emerged from a subject area that was limited by the field research you conducted; the information you were able to collect, analyze, and interpret; and the people you were able to collect it from. You had to ask yourself what kinds of claims you could make about your subject given the information you had and what parameters this material would set. In the course of drafting, you discovered what additional information you needed to collect. Also, as you wrote the essay, you were faced with choices about how to present the information—direct or indirect quotes, dialogue, or summary—how to identify the speakers, and how to present your connection to each of them.

For Essay 2, you will again gather information by talking to other people; however, this time, the topic you begin with as well as the focus you develop will be completely up to you. Such a wide-open choice may seem so vast as to be somewhat daunting, but zeroing in on such a seemingly unrestricted assignment provides valuable experience of the way writers actually work. Although some professional writing is the result of an assignment, the vast majority of it is created out of someone's desire to express an opinion, to answer a question, to provide some information, to propose a solution to a problem, and so on. Most writing evolves out of the writer's urge to say something.

It is true that the urge to say something is not the initial reason most students write. When you first enroll in some courses, you may feel you have no personal interest in the subject of study. You may be taking the course because you are required to; it may seem you have no reason for caring intellectually or personally about the assignments you are given. Further, most school writing assignments are contrived for the purposes of instruction. This text, too, asks you to go through a writing process that is somewhat artificial; you are doing assignments that we have designed in a particular way with particular intentions in mind.

While all work in school is in one sense an exercise, you will also find that some—perhaps a great deal—of your work in college will genuinely cause your world and your awareness to expand, will be meaningful not only for the skills or credentials it gives you to use in the future but for the experience it gives you now, in the present. To take full advantage of this experience requires making every subject you study, to some degree, your own, investing some of yourself in the assignments and the issues they raise.

The power that writing has to help people create a personal connection with their subject is the same power that helps them to figure out what they want to say or to clarify what they don't initially understand. In this sense, writing is a primary way to learn anything.

In the process of working on Essay 2, you will be using the exploratory writing activities you are already familiar with from the first assignment to write a second essay that is informed by the words, recollections, shared stories, observations, and commentary that you collect from other people. Though your instructor may ask you to include information from written texts or even personal memories, these will not be the primary sources for this essay. However, you will play a major role in the essay as the interpreter of the information you collect. Just as someone who reads many books and articles for a research paper must pull together and interpret what she or he reads, writers of this kind of essay must pull together and interpret what they hear and are told. This material then allows the writer to support and explain the meaning she wishes to convey.

THE ASSIGNMENT FOR ESSAY 2
Learning about a Subject of Your Choice by Observing and Listening

The general subject matter for the second essay can be any issue or concern that is currently on your mind. Once you have selected this topic, you will determine what particular focus your essay will take and what meaning you wish to convey to your reader. The only limitation on your selection is that the information you use to develop and support your ideas must come from observing and listening to others.

The following exploratory writing activities will help you identify your subject, find what you want or need to know about that subject, and determine what relevant information you can gather from listening to and observing others. As you reflect on this information, the activities will help you to find a focus for your draft and determine what additional information will help clarify your ideas and provide evidence for the points you wish to make.

You may want to review the student-written drafts in Chapter 14 to see how these writers develop their points and establish their support through the use of evidence gathered from listening and observing.

Exploratory Writing Activities for Creating Your Essay

The following writing activities include those you used in writing Essay 1, but we have arranged them in a different order, an order that reflects the kind of preparation you will need to do for this essay. Before beginning Essay 1, an essay for which the subject area was provided, you had already completed several reflections that had, in essence, been preparation for your draft. Since there is no subject matter provided for this essay, you will begin with your own concerns and questions to search for an area of interest for your essay. After finding a general subject, you will be guided through the exploratory writing activities that will help you explore the subject and find a specific topic or question, gather information, and find a focus for your essay.

1. Listing the Ideas That Interest You

As a way to begin, quickly list what is on your mind right now. You might ask yourself what questions and issues you are currently thinking about or struggling with. You might reflect on events currently in the news; articles or books you have recently read; situations at home, at school, or in the community; movies or performances you have recently seen; places you have visited; people in your life—don't feel that the list must be remarkable in any way other than that it provides a quick snapshot of some of what is going on in your mind at this time.

2. Selecting the Most Interesting Idea

Underline two items from your list that currently look most interesting. Write briefly—five to ten minutes—about each one. You can make your initial decisions on any basis you choose, narrowing down to the two items on the list that seem to be the most compelling thoughts or subjects, ones you would not mind giving a few minutes of your attention to today. The writing you do about each idea is expected to be unfocused and is intended to explore your knowledge, feelings, and state of mind about each item.

When you are finished, reread what you have written and select the item about which you have the most to say, the most curiosity, the greatest feeling, or even the greatest confusion.

3. Reflecting on Information

a. *What do you already know?* Thinking about the topic or question you have chosen, freewrite on what you already know about this topic. Describe what you know in detail. Tell about your current feelings and understanding.

b. *What do you need to know?* Write about what more you need to find out. What questions do you have? What do you want to know?

c. *How can you find out more?* Write down ways that you might find answers to the questions you listed in the previous step. Can you find out more about your topic by listening to people talk or by observing? What will you be looking for as you observe? What kinds of questions might you ask other people?

d. *What can you never know?* Write down the kinds of things that you could never understand about the topic. What is it that would prevent that understanding?

4. Gathering Information

a. Reread the three previous writings that you have just completed. Then, looking particularly at the last one, brainstorm some ideas about how you will collect this information and from whom. Don't limit yourself by reality—if anything were possible, to whom would you speak and what conversations would you want to overhear?

b. Brainstorm some more about information gathering, this time considering what you will actually be able to do and whom you will actually contact within the time limits of the assignment. Make a list of the people you will interview or have conversations with and the places you will visit to make observations. In order to make the process of gathering information most useful and productive, plan when would be the best time to make your observations and compose the questions you will ask.

Now use the next few days—or however long the assignment allows—to conduct your research, being sure to take complete and specific notes about what you hear or are told. Keep track of when you make your observations and the names of your speakers.

5. Questions and Connections

Once you have gathered the material you need, review all your data from your notes about the interviews you conducted, conversations you had, and observations you made. Reflect on the data to see what patterns may be emerging. What tentative conclusions can you draw from your material so far? What connections can you make? What thoughts do you have about what is meaningful in the information you have? Write three or four sentences about possible connections and patterns the data may suggest and conclusions you may be able to draw so far. At this point, what can you say about your topic? What would you like to know more about? Are there specific aspects of the topic that are of most interest to you? You might also put these thoughts into the form of a question to which you would like to find an answer.

6. Writing About the Ideas You Have Selected

Use the statement or question that you wrote in the previous step as a focus from which to begin this freewriting. Push yourself to write two or three pages. The only parameters are those set by the sentences you have already written.

7. Identifying an Emerging Focus for Your Essay

Skim through all of the pages you have written in these activities, paying special attention to the writing you completed for activity 5 about the topic for your essay. Make a determination about what explicit focus your first draft will have in relation to this topic. While this focus is likely to shift or evolve as you write and collect more data, at this moment, before starting a first draft, what claims do you want to make or points do you want to argue? What interpretation of your data do you want to present?

Write a couple of sentences that identify what it is that you want to be writing about. What in the data you have collected will be useful to you for this focus? What does the data tell you or what do you want to use the data to say?

8. One More Chance to Gather Information

Evaluate the information you have gathered in relation to the focus of your essay and the meaning you want to convey to your reader; from this determine what more data you need; ask yourself what additional field research you could do. There may be questions that occur to you after you review your notes that you didn't think of when you were first gathering information. There may be a place you need to visit again or additional people with whom you need to speak. Keep in mind that as you draft and revise, you can always pause at other points, as well, to collect whatever seems to be missing.

9. Visual Thinking

As a final activity before starting your first draft, make a brief sketch, diagram, or design in which you remind yourself of what is, so far, the focus of your essay and the claim you will make. Then, in whatever visual format works for you, arrange the information or data you have selected to help you make your points convincing and supportive of your claim.

Writing a First Draft of Your Essay

Using the focus that you have identified and drawing on the information or data that you have gathered, write a first draft of an essay in which you make your initial attempt to present and support the claim you have set out for yourself.

Because this is a college essay, by the time you finish revising your drafts, the point of the essay should be explicitly clear to the reader, and the information you have gathered should develop or support that point. However, because this is an early draft, don't worry too much yet about the correctness or completeness of what you are writing. There will be time for you to change sentences, rearrange ideas, and add or delete information later.

Once your draft is complete, you and your classmates can use the guidelines in Chapters 15 and 16 to revise and edit your draft as you move toward completing the final revision for your instructor.

CHAPTER
10

Essay 3: Learning About Writing from Recollections and Memories

Writing from Recollected Experiences

We want to make a distinction between writing *about* recollections and memories and writing *from* recollections and memories. In autobiographical writing, authors write about their recollections. Telling the autobiographical story is the focus of the piece of writing. In an academic essay, the writer uses recollections in the same way she would use a book in the library, as a source of information that provides evidence to support a point—and the point may or may not be about the author. In other words, because you are writing an academic essay, you will be writing *from* experiences you recall, in this case, about writing and learning. Just as in the previous essays you wrote *from* the information you gathered by talking and listening to what others said, here, your own writing and language experiences are a source of information, a place from which to find an issue to explore, questions to answer, and claims on which to focus your writing. While there are any number of ways your essay might evolve, it must have several features: it must include sustained reflective analysis of a subject or idea, convey an explicit meaning to the reader, and rely on your personal recollections and memories as its primary means of explanation and support.

THE ASSIGNMENT FOR ESSAY 3
Learning About Writing from Recollections and Memories

The general topic for this essay is writing, or learning to write, or learning language, and the source of information will be your own recollections and memories. It will be up to you to determine what particular focus your essay will take and what meaning you wish to convey to your reader. To help you, we will guide you through an analysis of some of the reflections you completed earlier. Once you determine your focus, you will use the information you have already gathered and additional information you will gather to provide evidence and support for your ideas.

36 Reflection
Learning from Students' Drafts

During the process of drafting this essay, turn to those essays in Chapter 14 that take their shape and direction from the particular recollections of the writer. Any one of these essays might have begun as yours will, with a writer reflecting on particular experiences. The writer then stood back from those initial recollections or feelings and analyzed them for repeated behaviors, points of conflict, or particular moments that could be understood or interpreted in particular ways. From this analysis grew the writer's own focus or reason for writing—to illustrate something about him/herself or someone else, to make an argument, to make a comparison, or to show a change. Just like your essay, each of these essays relies on the writer's own personal experience as a primary source of information. Each one uses this information to explain the point the writer wants to make, to support the claims that the writer is proposing.

Read these essays, noticing the various choices these writers made. Then answer the questions that we have embedded in each one.

Exploratory Writing Activities for Creating Your Essay

You will notice that the exploratory writing activities appear in the same order as you encountered them in the first essay. As with that essay, you have already begun your data collection, generating lots of relevant information in your reflections, which will be the first place we'll ask you to look for new or unfamiliar perspectives. We will also give you, in the course of the writing activities, time to reflect on what you have written and to recall and generate more data for the essay.

1. Questions and Connections

Reread the reflections that you completed in Chapters 4 and 5. Make some notes about any connections you see among them. You might consider questions such as: Can you make connections between your memories of writing experiences and your starting point as you began this course? What connections do you notice among the writing memories? Do the writing courses that exist on your campus meet your expectations for what college writing should be? How do your expectations, hopes, and fears about college writing fit with the expectations implied by the writing requirements at your school? What questions arise for you from the similarities and differences between your experiences and those of other students? Are there one or more reflections that seem particularly intriguing to you about which you may have more to say? You may be able to make many other connections that are not referred to in these questions.

2. Conflicting Points of View

Create a dialogue between two different points of view that emerge from your reflections. These differences may appear in your own recollected experiences or in the perspectives that you heard raised by others in the class.

Write a second dialogue that evolves differently than the first. Then, reread what you have written and write your reflection on these dialogues.

3. Metaphoric Thinking

Identify a concept or issue that appears in or is suggested by the writing, and write out two or three comparisons between the original concept and something that seems appropriate. (For example, writing in school is like . . . ; using computers to write is like . . . ; school newspapers are like . . . ; and so on.) Next, explain these comparisons. Write for a few minutes about how a comparison works, looking for what the comparison shows you about the concept that you might not have otherwise noticed.

4. Listing Ideas That Interest You

Reread the assignment and the first three exploratory writing activities. Quickly list the subjects that interest you so far by asking yourself what questions and issues your thinking about language and learning about language have raised for you. What bothers or interests you? What would you most like to know more about? This list provides a quick snapshot of some of what is going on in your mind in relation to the assignment at this time.

5. Selecting the Most Interesting Idea

Underline two items from your list that currently look most inviting. Write briefly—five to ten minutes—about each one. You can make your initial decisions on any basis you choose, narrowing down to the two items on the list that seem to be the most compelling subjects, ones you would not mind giving a few minutes of your attention to today. The writing you do about each idea is expected to be unfocused and is intended to explore your knowledge, feelings, and state of mind about each item.

When you are finished writing, reread these two brief writings and select the one about which you have the most to say, the most curiosity, the greatest feeling, or even the greatest confusion.

6. Identifying an Emerging Focus for Your Essay

Skim through all of the pages you have written in these activities, paying special attention to the writing you completed in activity 5 about a particular subject for your essay. Now, determine what explicit focus your first draft will have in relation to this subject. Expect this focus to shift and evolve as you write and collect more data. At this moment, before starting the first draft, what focus do you anticipate it will have? What meaning do you want to convey or what points do you want to argue?

Once you have written a couple of sentences that identify what this focus will be, look at the data or information you have gathered so far. What in the data that you have collected will be useful for conveying this focus? What does the data tell you or what do you want to use the data to say?

7. Reflecting on the Information

a. *What do you already know?* Thinking about the topic you have chosen, freewrite on what you already know about this topic. Describe what you know in detail. Tell about your current feelings and understanding.

b. *What do you need to know?* Write about what more you need to find out. What questions do you have? What do you want to know?

c. *How can you find out more?* Write down ways that you might find answers to the questions you listed in the previous step. Can you find out more about your topic by recollecting events and experiences from your past? What kinds of events are you searching for?

d. *What can you never know?* Write down the kinds of things that you could never understand about the topic. What is it that would prevent that understanding?

8. Gathering More Information

Considering the focus of your essay and reviewing the writing you have done so far, what more information do you need? What additional research do you need to do?

There may be certain kinds of recollections you need to bring to mind or have friends or family help you recall in detail.

9. Visual Thinking

As a final activity before starting your first draft, make a brief sketch, diagram, or design in which you remind yourself of what is, so far, the focus of your essay and the claim you will make. Then, in whatever visual format works for you, arrange the information or data you have selected to help you make your points convincing and supportive of your claim.

Writing a First Draft of Your Essay

Using the focus that you have identified and drawing on the information or data that you have gathered, write a first draft of an essay in which you make your initial attempt to present and support the claim that you have set out for yourself.

Because this is a college essay, by the time you finish revising your drafts, the point of the essay should be explicitly clear to the reader, and the information you have gathered should develop or support that point. However, because this is an early draft, don't worry too much yet about the correctness or completeness of what you are writing. There will be time for you to change sentences, rearrange ideas, and add or delete information later.

Once your draft is complete, you and your classmates can use the guidelines in Chapters 15 and 16 to revise and edit your draft as you move toward completing the final revision for your instructor.

CHAPTER

11

Essay 4: Learning About a Subject of Your Choice from Recollections and Memories

Reconsidering the Process of Writing

As you worked your way through Chapters 4 and 5, you paid attention to your past and present experiences with writing and learning, and to the relationships among these experiences. We limited your choice of subject matter for the third essay to topics that emerged from your reflections on writing and learning to write. Using the exploratory writing activities that started in your reflections, you composed an essay that drew on your own experience and observations: an essay that had an explicitly focused claim related to your thinking about writing.

Because personal knowledge can provide valuable information for college writing, we have designed the next assignment for further practice in reflecting on and analyzing your own experience. While you will again use personal experience as your data or information source for the essay, this time the subject matter of your essay has no limits—your essay may come from recollections and interpretations of *any* of your experiences. The exploratory writing activities will help you to examine and find a shape for your material, to make connections, observations, and interpretations, to learn what it is your experiences may be urging you to write, and to choose among these possibilities for a topic as well as a focus for your essay. Because the primary source of information for this essay is your analysis of recollected experiences, as it was in Essay 3, the memories and stories you recollect are the data from which a topic and, ultimately, a focus for your essay will emerge. At the same time, these recollections are the sources you will analyze and cite in your essay.

The following exploratory writing activities provide ways for you to think about and learn from new material you are studying and from any of your own experiences. The activities will help you to begin focusing in on a topic to examine in an essay.

When you scroll through your memory for experiences that might serve as the catalyst for this essay, consider especially those that are in some ways still unresolved, or those that have stayed with you, or that you find yourself thinking about. They need not seem important from the outside, or they may be. Use this writing assignment to think about things you are actually interested in thinking about. Working writers begin at this point, knowing they have something that, for them, needs to be written.

THE ASSIGNMENT FOR ESSAY 4
*Learning About a Subject of Your Choice
from Recollections and Memories*

The general subject matter for this essay will be any issue or concern that is currently on your mind, and the source of information will be your own recollections and memories. It will be up to you to determine what particular focus your essay will take and what meaning you want to convey to the reader.

The exploratory writing activities will help you identify your subject, find out what you want or need to know about that subject, determine what relevant information you can gather from your own recollections and memories, find a focus for your draft, and determine what additional information will provide the supportive evidence you need.

Writing Activities for Creating Your Essay

Because this essay, like Essay 2, did not begin with a series of writing reflections, we have reorganized the writing activities to help you to generate ideas, see what is on your mind, and find possible subjects that you can then examine from various perspectives.

1. Listing the Ideas That Interest You

As a way to begin, quickly list what is on your mind right now. Ask yourself what questions and issues you are currently thinking about or struggling with. Consider events currently in the world or national news, or articles or books you have recently read; situations at home, at school, or in the community; movies or performances you have recently seen; places you have visited; people in your life—don't feel that the list must be remarkable in any way other than that it provides a quick picture of some of what is going on in your mind at this time.

2. Selecting the Most Interesting Ideas

Underline two items from your list that currently look most interesting. Write briefly—five to ten minutes—about each one. You can make your initial decisions on any basis you choose, narrowing down to the two items on the list that seem to be the most compelling thoughts or subjects, ones you would not mind giving a few minutes of your attention to today. The writing you do about each idea is expected to be unfocused and is intended to explore your knowledge, feelings, and state of mind about each item.

When you are finished writing, reread these two brief writings and select the one about which you have the most to say, the most curiosity, the greatest feeling, or even the greatest confusion.

3. Reflecting on Information

a. *What do you already know?* Thinking about the subject you have chosen, freewrite on what you already know about this topic. Describe what you know in detail. Tell about your current feelings and understanding.

b. *What do you need to know?* Write about what more you need to find out. What questions do you have? What do you want to know?

c. *How can you find out more?* Write down ways that you might find answers to the questions you listed in the previous step. Can you find out more about your topic by searching your past experiences or recalling past relationships or events? What will you be looking for as you search?

d. *What can you never know?* Write down the kinds of things that you could never understand about the subject. What is it that would prevent that understanding?

4. Gathering Information

a. Reread the three previous writings that you have just completed. Then, looking particularly at the last one, brainstorm some ideas about how you will collect this information and from whom. Don't limit yourself by reality—if anything were possible, what events would you try to recall and with whom would you talk to help with the details?

b. Brainstorm some more about information gathering, this time considering what you will actually be able to do and whom you will actually contact within the time limits of the assignment. Make a list of the kinds of events you need to recall (School experiences? Work experiences? Family events? Others?) and people you will have conversations with to help you recall the details of your recollections. Now use the next few days—or as much time as the assignment allows—to conduct your research, being sure to take complete and specific notes about what you remember and any conversations you have that add to the details of these recollections.

5. Questions and Connections

Once you have gathered the material you need, review all your data from your notes. Reflect on the data to see what patterns may be emerging. What tentative conclusions can you draw from your material so far? What connections can you make? What thoughts do you have about what is meaningful in the information you have? Write three or four sentences about the connections and patterns you see and the conclusions you draw so far. At this point, what can you say about your topic? What would you like to know more about? You might also put these thoughts into the form of a question to which you would like to find an answer.

6. Writing About the Ideas You Have Selected

Use the statement or question that you wrote in the last activity as a focus from which to begin this freewriting. Push yourself to write two or three pages. The only parameters are those set by the sentences you have already written.

7. Identifying an Emerging Focus for Your Essay

Read through all of the pages you have written in these activities, paying special attention to the writing you completed for activity 5 about the topic for your essay. Now determine what explicit focus your first draft will have in relation to this topic. While this focus is likely to shift and evolve as you write and collect more data, at this moment, before starting a first draft, what do you want your essay to accomplish?

Write a couple of sentences that identify what it is that you want to be writing about. What in the data you have collected will be useful to you for this focus? What does the data tell you or what do you want to use the data to say?

8. One More Chance to Gather Information

Evaluate the information you have gathered in relation to the focus you have in mind and determine what more you need; ask yourself what additional field research you could do. There may be questions that occur to you after you review your notes that you didn't think of when you were first gathering information. There may be a place you need to visit to jog your memory or additional people with whom you need to speak. Keep in mind that as you draft and revise, you can always pause at other points, as well, to collect whatever seems to be missing.

9. Visual Thinking

As a final activity before starting your first draft, make a brief sketch, diagram, or design in which you remind yourself of what is, so far, the focus of your essay. Then, in whatever visual format works for you, arrange the information or data you have selected to help make your essay convincing.

Writing a First Draft of Your Essay

Using the focus that you have identified and drawing on the information you have gathered, write a first draft of an essay in which you make your initial attempt to present and support your ideas.

Because this is a college essay, by the time you finish revising your drafts, the focus of your essay and the points you are making should be explicitly clear to the reader, and the information you have gathered should develop or support your points. However, because this is an early draft, don't worry too much yet about the format and wording of what you are writing. There will be time for you to change sentences, rearrange ideas, and add or delete information later.

Once your draft is complete, you and your classmates will use the guidelines in Chapters 15 and 16 to revise and edit your draft as you move toward completing the final revision for your instructor.

CHAPTER 12

Essay 5: Learning About Academic Disciplines from Written Texts

Learning About an Academic Discipline

In addition to writing textbooks for students, we also have coauthored academic articles for professional journals. Since we work and live about three hundred miles away from one another, the process of writing together, which could be very difficult, has been made easier not only because we can send our drafts back and forth electronically but because we both know and use a common set of writing conventions. In earlier chapters, we mentioned that scholars in each discipline or subject area study topics in characteristic, conventional ways. Like the two of us, scholars in any given discipline work at universities and colleges across the country—and in other countries as well. So, when they want to have discussions with one another about their ideas and points of view, or they want to write together about these ideas, they do not merely walk across the hall, pick up the telephone or go online. They rely on the conventions of academic writing, which provide a common language or way of talking, thinking, and writing about ideas. For example, when we have written articles together, many decisions about how we would write had already been made by the conventions of our discipline. That is, we are both familiar with the sources of evidence that are expected in our discipline, the way others expect our arguments to be structured, the kind of writing style that is conventionally accepted by journals, and so on. For if our ideas are to be published and shared with other colleagues, we must write about them in a way that invites others in our discipline to join in the debate. This is the role of academic writing—to present and continue in a public forum the discussion and debate that begins privately. This is the reason instructors use academic texts as the primary sources for teaching students about the most significant debates occurring in a given discipline.

By *academic texts*, we mean the written materials that are respected by a community of scholars in a given discipline. These texts can be print journals (magazines published for academics and available through libraries or online), online journals, or educational websites. The means by which these texts are evaluated is similar to the guidelines we have already mentioned for websites. The location of the publisher is very important; often, publishers who work through universities or national academic organizations are most respected.

In your own college or university, disciplines are represented by individual academic departments or majors: history, English, communication, women's studies, environmental studies, computer science, mechanical engineering, and so on. The reflections you completed in Chapters 6 and 7 asked you to begin exploring the conventions of particular disciplines or departments by examining the courses and their requirements, by speaking with an instructor, and by looking closely at course materials and assignments. Now, we would like you to complete this exploration of a discipline using the third source of information available to writers: written texts.

THE ASSIGNMENT FOR ESSAY 5
Learning About Academic Disciplines from Their Written Texts

Like Essays 1 and 3, the subject matter of this essay is writing. The topic for this essay will be one that you select based on your review of writing done by academics in a particular discipline. Choose either the discipline in which you intend to major or another academic area you would like to learn more about. This assignment gives you an occasion to find out how academics in a particular discipline represent their ideas in their writing. It will be up to you to determine what specific focus your essay will take and what meaning you want to convey to your reader. Use the reflection and the exploratory writing activities that follow to gather and analyze the information that will help you focus your essay.

Once you determine that focus, the reflections in Chapters 6 and 7 and the one that follows, as well as relevant academic texts (journals, online resources, books), will provide supportive evidence for developing your essay.

37 Reflection
Identifying the Conventions of Academic Texts and Explaining Them in a PowerPoint Presentation

Work with several students in your class who share your interest in a particular major or group of related majors. Your group will examine the writing of academics in that particular discipline or disciplines and the writing students do in a related major or majors. Examine several relevant academic journals and prepare an electronic presentation, using a program such as PowerPoint, that explains and illustrates the characteristics of writing in the discipline(s) you are investigating.

To select the academic journals, review the interviews you had with instructors and the preliminary observations you made about academic journals in Reflections 30 and 31. Use your campus library or its Internet resources to select more journals to examine. To determine what kind of writing is required in the major, review Reflections 32 and 33. You can find out more about particular courses and their writing requirements by researching your school course catalog, website, or similar departmental materials. The following questions can guide your research and your presentation:

1. What topics seem to be most common in each journal?
2. How long are the essays on average?
3. What documentation style is required and what distinguishes this style?
4. What kind of information is cited?
5. How would you characterize the writing style of the essays?
6. How are essays submitted and selected?
7. From where is the journal published?
8. What kinds of writing assignments are most common in the courses in the major?
9. Are any writing assignments done collaboratively?
10. What stylistic preferences do there seem to be for writing in this major?

Exploratory Writing Activities for Creating Your Essay

The exploratory writing activities appear in the same order as you encountered them in Essay 1 and Essay 3. As you did when you worked on these essays, you have already begun your data collection for Essay 5, generating lots of relevant information in your reflections. So, the reflections will be the first place we ask you to look for new or unfamiliar perspectives. In the course of the writing activities, we will also ask you to take time to reflect on what you have written and to recall and generate more data for the essay.

1. Questions and Connections

Reread the reflections that you completed in Chapters 6 and 7 and think about the presentations that you and your classmates created. Make some notes about any connections you see among this material. Consider questions such as: What connections can you make between writing in a major and the scholarly writing in a discipline? How does the writing required of students differ from or seem similar to the writing in academic journals in that discipline? What questions arise for you from analyzing the rhetorical and stylistic conventions of academic writing in a particular discipline? What is distinctive about the questions and topics that are written about and the kinds of evidence that are most frequently used in a particular discipline? What might the evidence of academic texts suggest about what it means to think like a (historian, psychologist, microbiologist, and so forth)?

2. Conflicting Points of View

Create a dialogue between two different points of view that emerge from your reflections. These differences may appear in your own reflections, in the perspectives that you heard raised by others in the class, or in the academic journals you read.

Write a second dialogue that evolves differently than the first. Then, reread what you have written and write your reflection on these dialogues.

3. Metaphoric Thinking

Identify a concept or issue that appears in or is suggested by the academic texts you read, and write out two or three comparisons between the original concept and something that seems appropriate. Next, explain these comparisons. Write for a few minutes about how the comparison works, looking for what the comparison shows you about the concept that you might not have otherwise noticed.

4. Listing Ideas That Interest You

Reread the assignment for Essay 5 and the first three exploratory writing activities. Quickly list the areas of interest you have for the paper so far by asking yourself what questions and issues your thinking about the discipline and its writing and research raises for you. What bothers or interests you? What would you most like to know more about? This list provides a quick picture of some of what is going on in your mind in relation to the assignment at this time.

5. Selecting the Most Interesting Ideas

Underline two items from your list that currently look most interesting. Write briefly—five to ten minutes—about each one. You can make your initial decisions on any basis you choose, narrowing down to the two items on the list that seem to be the most compelling thoughts or subjects, ones you would not mind giving a few minutes of your attention to today. The writing you do about each idea is expected to be unfocused and is intended to explore your knowledge, feelings, state of mind about each item.

When you are finished, reread these two brief writings and select the one about which you have the most to say, the most curiosity, the greatest feeling, or even the greatest confusion.

6. Identifying an Emerging Focus for Your Essay

Read through all of the pages you have written in these activities, paying particular attention to the writing you completed in activity 5 about a particular subject for your essay. Now, determine what explicit focus your first draft will have in relation to this subject. Expect this focus to shift and evolve as you write and collect more data. At this moment, before starting a first draft, what focus do you anticipate the paper will have? So far, what meaning do you want to convey with your essay? Write a couple of sentences that identify what it is that you want to be writing about. What in the data you have collected will be useful for this focus? What does the data tell you or what do you want to use the data to say?

7. Reflecting on the Information

   a. *What do you already know?* Thinking about the topic you have chosen, freewrite on what you already know about this topic. Describe what you know in detail. Tell about your current feelings and understanding.

   b. *What do you need to know?* Write about what more you need to find out. What questions do you have? What do you want to know?

   c. *How can you find out more?* Write down ways that you might find out answers to the questions you listed in the previous step. Can you find out more about your questions?

   d. *What can you never know?* Write down the kinds of things that you could never understand about the topic. What is it that would prevent that understanding?

8. Gathering More Information

Considering the focus of your essay and reviewing the writing you have done so far, what more information do you need? What additional research do you need to do? You may need to locate more academic writing from the library or Internet.

9. Visual Thinking

As a final activity before starting your first draft, make a brief sketch, diagram, or design in which you remind yourself of what is, so far, the focus for your essay. Then, using whatever visual format works for you, arrange the information or data you have selected to help you make your points convincing and supportive of your claim.

Writing a First Draft of Your Essay

Using the focus that you identified earlier and drawing on the information or data that you have gathered, write a first draft of an essay in which you make your initial attempt to present and support the claim that you have set out for yourself.

Because this is a college essay, by the time you finish revising your drafts, the meaning you want to convey should be explicitly clear to the reader, and the information you have gathered should develop it. However, because this is an early draft, don't worry too much yet about the correctness or completeness of what you are writing. There will be time for you to change sentences, rearrange ideas, and add or delete information later.

Once your draft is complete, you and your classmates can use the guidelines in Chapters 15 and 16 to revise and edit your draft as you move toward completing the final revision for your instructor.

CHAPTER 13

Essay 6: Using Academic Texts to Inform Your Thinking

How Academic Writers Do Research

Although the kind of data or information that is valued varies from discipline to discipline, all academic areas respect the authority of written texts. In fact, much of the writing academics do uses written academic texts to support and develop our own arguments or ideas. The process of doing research actually begins when the hunches, questions, and conflicts that arise for us in the course of teaching, reading, observing, or talking with colleagues interest us enough to want to say something in response. But, in the academic world, one's credibility depends on framing one's responses within the context of what other academics have said that is related to the topic. So, before we can respond with our own observations and positions, we do library research, reading and taking notes from books and articles in order to become more familiar with the ideas and related discussions we will be responding to. Our purpose for doing this research is to find out what others have said, to learn what research has preceded our own, and in this way to find support for arguments we want to make, to become aware of arguments in opposition to our own, and to deepen and broaden our understanding of the subject we are studying. Research expands our thinking and leads us to look at our first ideas in a more informed and therefore more complex way. Research begins, then, with our own urge to respond to or extend the range of influence of something we have heard or read or seen, and it is motivated by our desire to inform, clarify, figure out, or strengthen what we have to say.

For the last assigned essay in *Writing Your Way Through College*, we would like to create for you this same kind of research experience and, as you did for Essay 5, use academic texts as your source of information. Starting with your own interests and recurring questions, you will use written academic texts as a source of information that can inform your thinking and provide the evidence necessary for writing this final essay.

THE ASSIGNMENT FOR ESSAY 6
Using Academic Texts to Inform Your Thinking

The subject for this essay will come from any issues that were raised for you by one of the first four essays you wrote. This previously written essay will serve as a starting point from which to write a new essay in which you add to your thinking about your subject by reading some related academic texts. From this reading and reflection, you will find a focus for your essay, and you will use the information you gather in the articles you read as evidence for the points you wish to make.

Because the focus of your essay and the evidence you will use to make your points will come from the academic texts you read, the ideas that you started with from the early essay may or may not play a role. That is, your earlier essay will serve as a springboard from which to create a new essay informed by the academic texts you will read.

---

38 Reflection
Learning from Students' Drafts

Once again, as you begin to draft your essay, we recommend that you turn to the student essays in Chapter 14. This time, look at the essay in which a student writer used information from academic texts for extending the ideas in her preceding essay. Read this essay carefully, noticing how the writer drew from others' texts as a way to focus and develop her own writing. To help you see the choices the writer made and their effects on the reader, answer the questions that we have embedded in the essay.

---

39 Reflection
Selecting the Essay from Which to Begin

Reread your Essays 1, 2, 3, and 4 and decide which of them you are going to use as the starting point for Essay 6. To make your decision, first freewrite for a few minutes about the essays and about what still interests, confuses, or intrigues you about each. What ideas remain unresolved for you? Using your freewriting, choose which of your essays contains ideas and points of view that you would like to explore further with the assistance of written academic texts.

40 Reflection
Locating the Academic Discipline in Which to Do Research

First, list the questions or issues that interest you in the essay you have chosen. What questions would you like to explore? Second, identify the academic discipline within which you are going to explore this question. Your instructor, classmates, and the library databases can help you to choose an appropriate discipline in which to gather information. Ask yourself what it is you want to find out and then ask (yourself or others) which academic disciplines might include scholarship on your topic. Using a library database, begin researching your topic. You are looking for anything academics have written that connects to ideas in your paper. As you find some of these connections, you can begin narrowing your focus to a much more specific dimension of the questions you addressed in your original paper. It is this much more specific focus that you will explain and support in your essay with evidence from the academic texts you are examining.

  As with other essays in this text, we will begin with drafting activities that will help you see what ideas, concepts, and questions you might like to consider for this final essay. The following activities will also provide ways for you to think about and learn from the texts you are reading and to begin focusing in on a topic for your essay.

Exploratory Writing Activities for Creating Your Essay

1. Listing the Ideas That Interest You

As a way to begin, quickly list what is on your mind right now, having reread your essay and having quickly read some related academic essays. Ask yourself what questions and issues you are thinking about or struggling with. What points are made in the articles that stand out for you? What points do you want to think about more? Don't feel that the list must be remarkable in any way other than that it provides a quick picture of some of what is going on in your mind at this time.

2. Selecting the Most Interesting Ideas

Underline two items from your list that currently look most inviting. Write briefly—five to ten minutes—about each one. You can make your initial decisions on any basis you choose, narrowing down to the two items on the list that seem to be the most compelling thoughts or subjects, ones you would not mind giving a few minutes of your attention to today. The writing you do about each idea is expected to be unfocused and is intended to explore your knowledge, feelings, and state of mind about each item.

When you are finished writing, reread these two brief writings and select the one about which you have the most to say, the most curiosity, the greatest feeling, or even the greatest confusion.

3. Reflecting on Information

a. *What do you already know?* Thinking about the subject or question you have chosen, freewrite what you already know about this topic. Describe what you know in detail. Tell about your current feelings and understanding.

b. *What do you need to know?* Write about what more you need to find out. What questions do you have? What do you want to know?

c. *How can you find out more?* Write down ways that you might find answers to the questions you listed in the previous step. What will you be looking for as you search?

d. *What can you never know?* Write down the kinds of things that you could never understand about the subject. What is it that would prevent that understanding?

4. Gathering Information

Use as much time as the assignment allows to conduct your research, being sure to keep track of your sources.

5. Questions and Connections

Once you have gathered the material you need, review all your data from your notes and the articles you read. What patterns do you see emerging? What conclusions do you draw from your material so far? What connections can you make? What ideas do you have about what is meaningful in the information you have? Write three or four sentences about the connections and patterns you see and conclusions you can draw so far. At this point, what can you say about your subject? What would you like to know more about? You might also put these thoughts into the form of a question to which you would like to find an answer.

6. Writing About the Ideas You Have Selected

Use the statement or question that you wrote in activity 5 as a focus from which to begin this freewriting. Push yourself to write two or three pages. The only parameters are those set by the sentences you have already written.

7. Identifying an Emerging Focus for Your Essay

Read through all of the pages you have written in these activities, paying particular attention to the writing you completed for activity 5 about a particular subject for your essay. Now, determine what explicit focus your first draft will have in relation to this subject. Expect this focus to shift and evolve as you write and collect more data. At this moment, before starting a first draft, what focus do you anticipate it to have? What do you want to convey with your essay?

Write a couple of sentences that identify what it is that you want to be writing about. What in the data you have collected will be useful to you for this focus? What does the data tell you or what do you want to use the data to say?

8. One More Chance to Gather Information

Evaluate the information you have gathered in relation to the meaning your essay is to convey and determine what more you need; ask yourself what additional data you might need. There may be questions that occur to you after you review your notes that you didn't think of when you were first gathering information. You may need to go back to certain journals or websites, reread certain articles, and add further information or evidence. Keep in mind that as you draft and revise, you can always pause at other points, as well, to collect whatever seems to be missing.

9. Visual Thinking

As a final activity before starting your first draft, make a brief sketch, diagram, or design in which you remind yourself of what is, so far, the focus of your essay and the claim you will make. Then, in whatever visual format works for you, arrange the information or data you have selected to help you make your points convincing and supportive.

Writing a First Draft of Your Essay

Using the focus that you have identified and drawing on the information or data that you have gathered, write a first draft of an essay in which you make your initial attempt to present and support your ideas.

Because this is a college essay, by the time you finish revising your drafts, the focus of your essay and the points you are making should be explicitly clear to the reader, and the information you have gathered should develop or support your points. However, because this is an early draft, don't worry too much yet about the format and wording of what you are writing. There will be time for you to change sentences, rearrange ideas, and add or delete information later.

Once your draft is complete, you and your classmates will use the guidelines in Chapters 15 and 16 to revise and edit your draft as you move toward completing the final revision for your instructor.

CHAPTER
14

Learning from Students' Drafts

Drafts That Use Observing and Listening as Their Source of Information

How Do You Say That in English?
By Brian McCoy

Three Americans are walking down a crowded Mexican street at dusk. As they make their way down the cobblestone street, a piercing steam whistle shatters the calm of the evening and causes nearby tourists to jump and shriek in surprise. Are they about to be run down by a train? One of the three unfazed Americans casually asks, "You wanna get some *camote*?" Just then a homemade metal pushcart rounds the corner into view, glowing red with heat and belching smoke.

Comment [1]: Why might the writer have chosen to include these particular details at the beginning of the essay?

What sets these three Americans apart from the tourists on the street? They are obviously not surprised by the steam whistle, and are even aware that the noise is merely a sweet potato vendor drumming up business. But why call it *"camote"* instead of just saying "sweet potato?" Why would a native English speaker choose to use a foreign word in an otherwise English sentence, especially considering that the intended audience also speaks English?

All of us belong to many different social groups. In our daily lives, we speak to family members, coworkers, and members of our bowling leagues or yoga classes. Each of these groups has its own unique way of using language, not only for communication but also to reinforce the sense of identity of that group. These language communities often coin new words, use existing words in new ways and create new expressions both to better describe the realities of life within the language community and to create a sense of belonging among the members of the community.

Comment [2]: As a reader, what is your reaction to this explanation?

Most language communities develop their unique vocabularies by drawing on a variety of sources within the community, such as simple imagination, technical jargon, or shared stories and experiences. However, a unique situation arises when speakers of one language from one culture have extensive contact with speakers of another language from a different culture. In this case, there is already a huge, readily available supply of words from the other language that can be used within the language community. In many instances, a conscious or unconscious blending of the two languages takes place when foreign words are borrowed into the normal daily vocabulary of the language community. Language communities of this type are seen among immigrant groups, exchange students, aid workers, expatriate communities, inhabitants of border areas, and virtually anywhere where a large amount of contact between speakers of different languages takes place.

Comment [3]: What has the writer said in this paragraph that brings to mind something from your own experience?

Speakers of one language who are living within another culture are often brought together in very close relationships by their feelings of isolation from the society around them, and these close relationships are frequently manifested in the development of a distinct form of language used within the transplanted community. This special language serves not only to bind community members together, but also to exclude those who are not part of the group. These attributes are not unique to language communities that borrow words from foreign languages, but are shared by language communities that exist in a variety of contexts.

Comment [4]: Some readers have told us that this paragraph is hard to read. Other readers feel that this paragraph is necessary and important to the essay. What arguments could be made for each point of view, and which one do you agree with?

I have personal experience in being a member of these transplant language communities, as a traveler in the Czech Republic and as a student in Mexico. In both instances, I became a part of distinct English-speaking language communities that evolved their own vocabularies and ways of speaking that incorporated a great many words borrowed from the local languages.

To give an example of how this sort of word borrowing occurs, I'll first take a piece from what would be a very normal conversation among exchange students in the Czech Republic. Imagine that your friend in Prague calls you up and gives you this invitation: "Do you want to go to the *pivnice* at the *námesti* by my house and get some *nakladany hermelin* and a couple of *dvanactkas*? Then maybe we can stop by the *potraviny* and pick up some *sekct* and take the *tramvaj* over to Samantha's." Would you want to go? If you were a member of this language community you would know that you were being asked to a sort of low budget tavern at the square by your friend's house to have cheese pickled in spicy onion oil (very tasty) and strong beer. Then you were going to the mom-and-pop grocery store to buy some Czech champagne and then taking the streetcar to Samantha's. If you were to listen in on a conversation among English teachers in Mexico, you might hear someone complaining: "I'm totally *encabronado.* I went down to the *migra* today to get my *efe eme tres*, and there were so many *tramites* and so much hassle that I finally realized that the guy was asking for a *mordida.* So I had to give it to him." If you were a member of that language community, you would know that your friend was pissed off because he had gone to the Immigration Office to get his green card, but there was so much paperwork and so many procedures that he ended up having to give the officer a bribe.

The question arises that if it is possible to express all of the ideas contained in these three examples in Standard English, why do members of these language communities feel the need to borrow foreign words? To answer this question, it is useful to examine exactly what types of words are borrowed. To form general categories, I first examined my own experiences using borrowed words, and then interviewed a few people about their experiences to see if the words they borrowed fell into these groups. I interviewed Mary, a former AFS student in Niger, Paul, another former AFS student who lived in Benin, and Dan, who lived in Ecuador as a missionary. The vocabulary that all four of us used seems to fall mostly into the categories of geographic features, types of businesses, food words, and general expressions.

Comment [5]: Why does the writer tell us where he got his information?

Geographic features and proper names of places are often used in speech within these communities, Words like "main square," "national theater," "town hall," and "courthouse" are easily learned through signs, maps, and names of transportation stops. Although these words can be translated, saying "main square" conjures up an image of some sort of American location, whereas *zócalo* gives a very specific mental picture of a Mexican main square. Speakers also use local words to describe locations that do not exist in the speakers' home country, such as *panelaky* to describe giant, prefab, Soviet era, concrete housing projects, or *chata* to describe a sort of shack in the Czech countryside where city dwellers go on the weekends to relax.

As well as knowing the word for the country shack, speakers also need to know the name of the store where you buy the supplies for your weekend in the country.

Regardless of where you are living, a great deal of your day-to-day life is spent buying things. Unfortunately, finding where to get the things you want is one of the hardest initial aspects of adjusting to a foreign culture. Not all countries have a readily accessible discount store where you can buy everything in one place. Many countries have entirely different systems of commerce with a variety of specialized shops not commonly found in the US. The names of these businesses are another source of vocabulary borrowing. What do you call a store that sells only paper products, from toilet paper to business cards? How about a store that sells only plastic products, or only smoked meats, or fruits and vegetables, or candy and pastries? How about a place that recycles tires, or makes made-to-order wrought-iron bars for windows and balcony railings? What do you call a man who sharpens knives door-to-door, or even something as simple as a mom-and-pop neighborhood grocery? We may be able to conjure up some word from the distant past like blacksmith, tinker or greengrocery to describe some of these businesses, but simply using the foreign word that is clearly printed on the sign outside gives a much more accurate mental picture.

Comment [6]: Why does the writer choose to provide multiple examples to illustrate his point?

Probably the most common category of word borrowing is food. This goes on a great deal even in Standard English, where words such as pizza, chow mein, sauerkraut, and hollandaise are understood by everyone. Food words are also some of the first vocabulary that foreigners learn in a new country, and therefore some of the first to be borrowed into their native language. If you want some big French fries made from yams *(dundu)* from a street vendor in Niger or some shredded beans *(gari)* in Benin, you need to learn the word, both so you can buy some and so you can tell your English-speaking friends about it later. The borrowed words may describe unfamiliar foods, such as Ecuadorian salty fried green banana chips *(chifles)*, Mexican fried grasshoppers cooked with hot chilies and onions *(chapulines),* or something as normal as mashed potatoes. The food becomes strongly associated with the word, and borrowing the word acts as a sort of mental short-cut in conversation.

Comment [7]: Notice the way the writer used information from his interview sources. How else might he have presented this information? What effect would the different presentations have made for you?

The fourth category of commonly borrowed words is general expressions. Expressions can be borrowed when they convey a sentiment that does not exist in English or is not easily translatable, or when the foreign expression is shorter or just has a nice ring to it. English speakers living in Niger may inject the Hausa expression, "*Sai hankuri fa*" into their speech, which means something like "have patience," or "that's just the way it is, there's nothing you can do about it," or, to use another borrowed expression, "*C'est la vie.*" This seems to be a concept lacking in English, because Dan also described using "*Asi a?*" to express this idea. To refer to someone as a "*yope*" among English speakers in Oaxaca, Mexico means that the person is a poor, indigenous peasant from some isolated village. Shouting out "*Kal?*" to another English speaker in Niger saves you the trouble of saying, "Hey, what are you doing?" or, "Don't touch that!" And for speakers in Benin, "*Wafi!*" is a quick and melodic way of saying, "Come here!"

These borrowed words are by no means universal among all English speakers living in these countries, but come into common use among close-knit groups of friends or co-workers as a way of establishing identity and of setting themselves apart from new arrivals, and worst of all, tourists. Knowledge of the language and culture is a form of social status in many cases, and new arrivals must quickly acquire new vocabulary in order to be accepted as an equal in the group and not as someone who must be educated.

Language: A Limiter of Communication

By Vanessa Rivera

I t's the big day. Droves of women hurriedly scamper to the counter. Some trot; some skip; others power walk or run to be the first in line. It's the opening day of Make-up Bonus Week at the mall. For those of you who are not familiar with make-up jargon, during busy bonus time, any purchase of $19.50 or above will yield you a free gift. This gift is usually small, consisting of a few trial-size items in some type of make-up bag or gift box. Since the brands of make-up that provide bonuses are usually on the pricey side, many women usually hold off on all their purchases until this time; they feel less guilty about buying something so expensive because they're getting something for free. I, of course, lover of free stuff that I am, was one of those women in the stampede. Whenever I embark on an adventure at a department store or at a more "classy" establishment, I try to always do two things: (1) dress like I am loaded (with money, of course), and (2) speak like I am actually articulate and highly-educated. This ritual evolved from many of my past experiences. Many a time I have tried to fool myself into thinking that how one looks or speaks makes no difference to the way one is perceived; but that is just not true. That is why it is an ideal and not the norm. The way one uses language is definitely a factor in how one is perceived; my observations have led me to believe that language—though supposedly the most essential vehicle for communication *is* actually a limiter, or barrier, of communication.

> **Comment [8]:** How does the writer indicate what the focus of her essay will be?

That day at the make-up counter, I observed many injustices due to language assumptions on the part of the sales clerks. As I waited patiently, I felt sorry for the older women whose English was not "standard enough." They stood in line like cattle at the slaughterhouse, waiting patiently for their turn to be chewed to pieces by 20 year old girls who were seemingly helpful but hiding behind the mask of "higher language." I witnessed as an older woman who spoke with an accent very similar to the one used by my own relatives struggled to ask about the anti-aging face cream.

"Hello, is this the cream that make you look young and skin is smooth? How much it is? I get free gift with this? What come in free gift?"

I glanced at the salesgirl; her face puckered up in future wrinkles that made her look like the famous horror-film clown's long lost sister. She was so visibly agitated that she grabbed the jar of anti-aging wonder and immediately started explaining—in her irate, preschool teacher manner—that the product would work for her wrinkles, that she would get her free gift, and (in layman's terms) to hurry up and get out of the store. I braced myself. I would be next. I tried to come up with more ornate verbiage that I could subtly sneak in between make-up jargon and questions about prices.

"Hi," the first salesgirl chirped to me, "have you been helped yet?"

"No, I have not."

"Ok, what can I get for you today?"

"I'd like your assistance in selecting a lipstick color that complements my skin tone. I am hoping to acquire one with pinkish-brown undertones."

"Sure, I'd love to help you with that. Are you also interested in getting the bonus? You might want to get a lip liner with that then. Let's go over here."

"Thank you; that would be lovely. I am quite pleased that you decided to assist me. Thank you for your prompt attention."

> **Comment [9]:** What about the way the writer spoke do you think caused the desired effect on the salesclerk?

On this particular day, I was relieved that I was able to use the way I spoke in order to get better service from the saleswoman. But I was also sad for the woman who was treated unfairly. In this example, language limited the communication between the saleswoman and the customer who did not speak "proper English." The older woman had a strong accent and perhaps was also unfamiliar with English sentence structure. The woman was also deemed "inferior"—whether consciously or subconsciously—by the saleswoman because she diverted from standardized English. The conversation was "hit and miss." The customer may have wanted more assistance or more information but because of her "improper" English, she was given less help. When I spoke with the salesgirl, I was given much more assistance than the woman who did not use Standard English. I was no more deserving of the help than the other woman was but because she preferred my language to hers she was kinder and more attentive to me. I suppose it was then that I deemed Standard English to be the "high" language and more simplistic, common speech (including slang), the "low" language. I found that although I was versed in both languages, I preferred the "high" language because I believed that I would be perceived as an educated person and therefore, respected. Still, I was disturbed by the fact that although language was supposed to help us communicate better with others, it was being used to limit our connection with people who were being treated as if they were inferior simply based on the language they spoke.

This communication discrimination is not limited only to people who speak the "low" language. On more than one occasion, I have witnessed people who spoke the "high" language discriminate against people who used "low" language. But I have also experienced the opposite. Earlier, I told you that I decided to make "high" language my everyday language of choice. I had many acquaintances who were used to hearing my "low" language; so when I began to speak to them in standardized English, the majority of them did not appreciate it.

"Hey Vanessa wussup?"

"Not much, how are you?"

"We cool. Man ain't there ever nothin' to eat up in this joint? You'all wanna kick back at my crib tonight?"

"I'm not sure; I have so many assignments tonight. Perhaps we could save that for another evening."

"Hey, what the hell is wrong with you? Got a stick up yo ass o somethin'? You talkin' like a white girl now? Oh what, you too good fo' us? Please."

These ex-friends of mine perceived my use of standard language as a threat. They believed that I was "selling out" or "acting white." Although I tried to tell them that trying to "speak properly" is not reserved for Caucasians but for anyone who would like to be able to speak to a wider audience, they continued to believe their assumptions. I was left with very few friends.

Language could be a very effective tool of communication if we do not readily make assumptions about it. We should also remember the purpose of language. What is it here for? What does it do? Language is supposed to be used to communicate with others. Too many times we are haughty about our language, and we decide that our language is the preferred one. That is unfortunate because we then create a barrier between "us" and "them." This

Comment [10]: What is the relationship that the writer is making between the point she just made and the one that she is about to make?

Comment [11]: What impact does the direct quote have on conveying the writer's point to the reader?

discrimination happens with people using both the "high" and the "low" languages. But we, being college students, should remember that we go to school to learn how to effectively communicate with many people, not just other students. Next time, when you come across someone who speaks from a different language community, just get off your high horse and try your best to understand.

Comment [12]: Sometimes writers use their evidence to change the way readers think or behave. To what extent are you persuaded by her evidence?

Extensive Restrictive Language
By Christy Ware

"Why did someone write SOB in my father's chart? I think that is a bit unfair," Mr. Adams stated. Assuming the initials stood for son of a bitch, the nurse quickly responded with the true definition of the written acronym SOB, shortness of breath. Many people will find the terminology the medical industry uses as difficult to grasp as a complicated foreign language. With thousands of words specific to the medical industry, it seems in many situations where dialogue exists in this field between medical professionals and those professionals and their clients, people are frequently meeting limitations due to time restraints, similar abbreviations, and the individuality of the speaker or receiver of information.

Comment [13]: What effect does the writer create by starting the essay with Adams' quote?

In an interview I conducted with Cindy Scalla, a Registered Nurse, she detailed a problematic situation involving acronyms in medical terminology. Cindy acknowledged the presence of similar abbreviations for different procedures. "PT" is used to describe physical therapy or it can also stand for prothromin time which measures the cloning factor in the individual. The doctor may order a PT or he may prescribe PT, and by altering only one word in the sentence, it may send the patient in the wrong direction and consequently the patient may suffer from this slight miscommunication.

Comment [14]: Notice that the writer identifies her source as a registered nurse. What is the effect of this information on the reader?

Cindy also confirmed another possibility involving miscommunication. Miscommunication can occur due to the time restrictions one must compete with in a hospital environment. For example, a doctor may give instructions in regards to a patient while completing multiple tasks, and he or she may order a PT quickly over the phone. The individual who received the doctor's instructions may have jotted them down hastily in an effort to get to their next patient or task and may have done so inaccurately. He or she may have stated "patient needs a PT," (prothromin time) instead of "patient needs PT" for physical therapy. The mistake would eventually be caught when the order for physical therapy is not found or signed by the doctor, but the waste of time and confusion has already occurred due to the lack of clarity and time constraints.

I witnessed a medical conference conversation with a patient's family where the medical language was misunderstood and caused tension and difficulty communicating different issues involving the patient. When the family confused the chart's notes containing the initials "SOB" with slang, instead of its intended meaning of shortness of breath, the family was upset. The nurse asked why the family was upset, and one family member replied that the initials they saw in the chart made them uncomfortable with the staff. Once the situation was clarified, the conversation took a positive turn and information was more readily shared between the family and staff. Although the misunderstanding was resolved, the miscommunication caused unnecessary delays in the meeting.

Comment [15]: Here the writer is reporting on what she heard from others. What assumptions do you make about how the writer conducted her research and gathered this information?

Even in a seemingly secure environment medical personnel may find that they are not free to discuss a subject openly because they don't wish to offend that person. Recently an article published on MSNBC indicated that a patient of a primary care physician filed a lawsuit against him for telling her she is obese. This patient was apparently offended by the alleged derogatory way he stated this fact. I don't believe there could be any easy way to relay this information to a patient especially when men and women can be very sensitive about their weight, even if they fall within the healthy guidelines set by the American Heart Association. Meanwhile, physicians, physician assistants, nurse practitioners, and nurses are instructed to inform their patients of the health risks associated with obesity, a category the Association refers to when a person's weight is above a set amount, yet some people are insulted if they are educated in a way that is inconsistent with their form of language. In sensitive situations it is increasingly difficult to discuss medical problems with patients in a language that patients will respond to positively.

After learning about this report, I spoke with Cindy again to inquire why, in her professional and experienced opinion, a case like this would arise. She informed me that it is possible the doctor had repeatedly and more delicately instructed the patient to lose weight and many times the client refuses to listen to the warnings given which may lead to a more direct form of communication between the physician and the patient. It is at those uncomfortable times that people who initially are unwilling to take the physician's advice may finally listen. At times, if the topic is something they would rather not hear, that person may become upset, as may be the case with the woman filing the lawsuit. I then considered in what way someone would listen to a doctor's advice without becoming offended. There is not an easy answer for everyone is different in the way they give and receive information, and those communication barriers cause problems in this industry.

Comment [16]: How does the writer use the person she is interviewing to help her expand on the point she made in the previous paragraph?

In many situations in the medical field, Scalla explained, she finds that she is restricted by language for she states she must continually add supportive sentences to further illustrate her thought, or when speaking to someone, she is constantly restating her original thought to emphasize or clarify a point. "Perhaps the doctor followed this process several times, but could not get across to his client the danger she was in, at which point he may have chosen to take a more direct route," Cindy elaborated. While the issue did get through to the client, it did not get there in an acceptable manner, or so this woman felt. It is clear that regardless of the language the medical industry uses, they are continually running into restrictions with effective communication.

Comment [17]: How does the writer help us to interpret the information she provides?

Recently I sprained several of my toes and was forced to visit the doctor's office. At the time of the visit, the doctor was unaware that in my part-time job I work in a hospital and am able to understand a bit of the language used there. Oblivious to my background, he spoke to me entirely in the language of wider communication. Not once did I hear him utter a medical term or abbreviation. This seamless shift the doctor made from medical language to the language of wider communication made me wonder why use this medical language at all? The information was relayed to me without once using medical terminology. Wouldn't it prevent misunderstandings and prevent certain individuals from becoming offended if this were always done?

Comment [18]: What is the effect on the reader that the writer makes observations from different perspectives of her life—as a patient in the hospital, an employee of the hospital, and a student of writing?

My four years of experience in the medical field brought me to the conclusion that it is accuracy and time management that is the basis for using this contrived language. I've found in my job the necessity to use medical terminology to quickly define a client's situation. For example, the term "stress incontinence" refers to the inability to get to the bathroom in a timely manner as to prevent a urine accident. Rather than saying my client is able to hold his or her urine as long as they are able to get to a commode or facility in a timely manner, I would use the term "stress incontinence" instead to quickly relay information. Despite the many restrictions and miscommunications found within the medical language, the availability of the terminology it provides is important to quickly define a person's diagnosis; unfortunately it does not help with effective communication between medical personnel and non-medical personnel.

Comment [19]: How does the writer's own data lead her to ask questions and provide answers?

The medical industry is concerned with language and the ability to communicate effectively as shown by doctor's business letters and medical websites that contain the statements, "please feel free to ask any question," or "please feel free to contact . . ." Although the doctors suggest open communication, rarely do many of their clients truly feel free to do so, and throughout the medical industry it appears that even with the adaptation of a complex, specialized language it is extremely difficult to communicate effectively.

Works Cited

Associated Press. "Doctor in Trouble for Calling Patient Obese." *MSNBC* 24 August 2005 <http://www.msnbc. msttcomJidI9O63638/>

Scalla, Cindy. Personal interview. 7 September 2005.

Lost in Translation
By Jennifer Swift

In the world of college writing, I feel that learning how to write academically is like learning a foreign language. The structure, conventions, and overall language that are expected in college writing evoke confusion and greatly intimidate me. While learning French, I have developed the same feelings towards this new language. Finding the right words to correctly express the meaning I am trying to convey is very difficult, and I often feel the purpose in my writing or speech gets lost. In French, and in college writing, I focus on translating my words correctly instead of focusing on the purpose of the conversation or piece of writing. By comparing my attempt at academic writing to my learning the French language, I can accurately portray how both languages feel foreign to me; even after all my schooling on the two subjects.

I have been in the process of learning languages, the language of writing and the French language, since I was five years old. Both are very intimidating at first, and it can be difficult to keep up. When I am in a group of people who are speaking French, I feel that by the time I understand the first few words, the conversation has moved on. During one of my French classes in high school, my teacher asked me, "Qu'est-que-ce? C'est une jupe rouge." By the time I could process the first question, she had already finished the second sentence. Processing the information and translating it, feels slow. In my senior writing class in high school, by the time I could master one concept, the class had moved on to another. I was never taught the proper way to write a paper in elementary school, so I found myself less advantaged than most of my peers. While learning how to form an essay, I was stuck struggling with the components of an introduction while my class had moved on to the body of the essay. As I move through college, and I write more and more papers, I still find myself struggling with the correct fit for the puzzle of words and phrases that I am expected to use. The difficulty of keeping up with my peers

Comment [20]: What does this writer do to draw the reader in to her essay? What else might she have done?

in both French and college writing adds to my feeling foreign to these languages.

When I am trying to express myself in French or write a college essay, it is difficult to choose which words demonstrate the true meaning I am trying to express. When speaking or writing in French, words may mean one thing in English, but when they are translated into French, they mean a completely different thing. For example, *ami(e)* or *copain(e)* both mean friend, but if you use these words in a different context, they can mean boyfriend or girlfriend. I often struggle with which words to use in different situations. When I am translating my conversational speech into the language of college writing, I seem to have the same problem. The words I tend to use do not mean what I am trying to express. I often look words up in a thesaurus and choose the wrong synonym, or I rearrange the words in a sentence to try and make it appear better, instead of helping, these attempts merely confuse the reader. The meaning and purpose in my writings get lost in the sea of confusing words, phrases, and conventions I am expected to use. For both French and college writing, not knowing which words to use often makes my speech or writing awkward and unclear.

Comment [21]: How does the writer use what she says in her essay to extend the ideas about writing that are explained in the textbook?

Something as simple as taking my thoughts and translating them into words, proves to be a very difficult task for me. In my French 101 class, I had to create a Power Point presentation that described a particular province of France. I had translated my words into French incorrectly, and my teacher had to pick apart every word I wrote to find out what I truly meant. In the first essay I wrote for this class, I had my sister proofread my first draft of the paper. I had to explain to her what I was trying to say in each sentence because my meaning was lost and the words I chose were confusing. After the first paragraph, she asked, "So what's the point of the paper? I don't get what point you're trying to make?" Obviously I had not translated my idea for my thesis onto paper in a clear and explicit way. In both situations, my purpose for writing got lost as I translated my thoughts into words.

Comment [22]: What effect does the writer create by citing two examples to support her point?

Learning to fit in and feel comfortable in a language situation is a task of its own. When I am with a group of fluent French speakers, I feel as though everyone can look at me and know I do not fit in. I may be familiar with the language, but I don't fit in with the culture and manner in which they carry themselves. This same concept of "not fitting in" applies to my feelings towards college writing as well. Selecting an appropriate voice for my writing is tied to the perspective and voice I take on myself as a writer. Because I do not feel confident about myself as a writer, the voice I create for myself is one of not fitting in, of doubt, fear, and uncertainty.

After talking with some of my peers, I found that they seem to fit in with the writing community much better than I do. One of my classmates, William, enjoys writing and feels he is a good writer with a good style of communication. Although I can attempt to learn the language of writing in general, the voice I take on doesn't feel like my own. It feels like I am trying to be something that I am not, a good writer. Even though I have been learning these two languages for a very long time, I do not feel like I fit in, I still feel foreign to them. Much like Rita E. Negion Maslanek explains about her move from Puerto Rico to America, "learning a new language [is] the easy part. Learning to fit in [is] the bigger challenge" (Maslanek, 39).

As I have entered the world of college writing, learning to situate myself in this community, just like in my French language community, is a gradual process. From the day I entered college I have been learning the conventions, rules, and language I need to continue writing and speaking appropriately in these communities. With time, maybe my brain will retain the information I need, and I will feel comfortable with college writing rather than like I am trying to write in a different language. By the time I finish my college education, I hope to have mastered the tools I need so my purpose for writing is no longer lost in translation.

> **Comment [23]:** Although the writer primarily uses personal experience as the source of data for her essay, she briefly refers to a text that she read and a conversation that she had to add to her evidence. How did that additional evidence affect you as you read?

Works Cited

Maslanek, Rita E. Negion. "Bayamon to Brooklyn." In *Language Crossings: Negotiating the Self in a Multicultural World*. NY: Teachers College Press, 2000, 35–39.

Walk, Don't Run

By Angela Bisceglia

As a child, I spent my summers at swim camp. Every day I would put on my uniform of red shirt and blue shorts, ride the short distance to camp in the back of our family van, and join my fellow campers. In the mornings we would spend our time running on the playground, playing tag or hide and seek. The sun would be high in the sky, beating down on us, soaking our skin with its heat. After lunch we would all line up with our towels in hand, and prepare for the walk to the pool. It was a long walk, the path had many twists, turns, and steep hills. But none of that mattered because we knew that very soon we would plunge into the salvation of the cool water.

Comment [24]: At this point in the essay, what do you imagine this essay will be about, and what in the first paragraph is indicating that to you?

Once we arrived at the pool, my friends and I would scramble to kick off our shoes and pull off our clothes, revealing the bathing suits underneath. We couldn't wait to jump into the pool. The anticipation could be seen in our little faces. My favorite game was to run jumps off the diving board, splashing into the pool, the cool water all around me. But I knew that before I could run and jump, before I could swim at all, the camp director would make us line up along the fence at the shallow end and recite the rules of the pool: "1. No yelling; 2. No going to the bathroom in the pool; 3. No beginners in the deep end; 4. No horseplay; 5. Walk, don't run."

Looking back, it was the last rule that always bothered me. I could not understand what the camp director was warning me about. Why would she want us to walk when we could run? I spent most of my day running around with my friends, and the pool was the best place ever so why in the world would she tell me not to run here? This was the activity that I waited for all day. I would have been happy without any of the other perks. I didn't need kickball; I could skip afternoon snack; and no naps for me—just let me go swimming! I can't even remember how many times the lifeguards had to remind me to "slow down" and how many times I sat in the plastic chair at the end of the pool, watching my friends swim because I had run, not walked. Yet no matter how many times I was "grounded," not many days would pass before I was busted one more time for moving too quickly and not following the rule.

Comment [25]: As readers, what do we come to understand about the writer from the personal experiences that she integrates into this part of the essay?

As I grew older, the difficulty of following the rule did not go away. In elementary school, when we had math problems, I would do the problems as quickly as possible and rush to give my teachers the answers. They would ask, "What steps did you take to get this answer?" I would say, "I don't know. I just knew it." But that wasn't good enough. The teachers made me redo the work, writing out each problem and showing the steps it took to get the answer. In my mind the teacher was saying, "Walk, don't run." Just like in swim camp, I could not understand why she would tell me this. As a teenager, I fought with my parents when they would give me a curfew or ask me to do household chores. "I'm old enough to make my own decisions," I would argue. My parents would respond, "We are just trying to help you on your way." Again, the voice in my head heard, "Walk, don't run." Why didn't my parents see that I was ready to conquer the world? I was confident that I could be successful on my own, and I didn't need to take time to listen to their advice or stories.

Although it took many reprimands from teachers and disagreements with my parents, I can now say that it has become my choice to "Walk, don't run." What was once a restriction has become a way of life. I have come to cherish every moment with my family and friends. I appreciate the slower pace and find that I experience life much more fully. The arguments that I once had with my parents have been replaced by long, meaningful conversations. I no longer see them as mean people who don't understand me and won't let me be my own person. They are now my best friends. But I was only able to change my view about them once I slowed down and took the time to get to know them.

Even though I have my own apartment, I try to visit my parents at least once a week, and last summer we even took a vacation together to visit my aunt and uncle in Portland. During the long car ride from California to Oregon, I asked lots of questions and heard lots of stories. By taking the time to sit with my parents and have a full conversation, I came to understand their point of view. I came to know them as individuals, not just my parents. I learned that they had lives before I became a part of their world. More importantly, I learned that the things they were trying to teach me came from mistakes they had made. They wanted me to learn from them and not make the same mistakes.

Comment [26]: Notice that this writer often uses briefly quoted lines to show us what she or other people in her story might have said. She could have conveyed this information without using a quote (for example, "My parents told me that they were just trying to help me on my way"). As a reader, what do you feel would be the difference between these two ways of writing?

Comment [27]: How do the examples in this paragraph parallel the first story the writer provided about swim camp? How do they extend the point she made there?

I have learned a lot about myself through these conversations with my parents. I can honestly say that we have a lot in common and that these similarities have helped to shape the person I am today. I know that my mother and I have the same dry sense of humor, but will both cry when we watch sappy movies or get mushy birthday cards. My father and I frequently forget that in a family debate, yelling the loudest does not mean that you win. In school my mother had the skill to excel in her classes, but was more interested in hanging out with her friends; I was the same. My dad was extremely athletic; in high school he was the star quarterback. I was also athletic and played as many sports as I could in school. I am cautious and uneasy about trying new things like my mother, but spend money freely like my dad.

Comment [28]: What impact does this series of comparisons that the writer makes in this paragraph have on you as a reader in relation to the claim she makes about her changed perspective?

I could only have come by this knowledge about myself by spending time with my parents, by taking the time to learn about them. When I was younger, moving at a faster pace, I was sure that I was different from them. There would have been no way that I would have considered myself even slightly similar to my parents. How could we be alike, I was a mover and a shaker; they barely left the house.

What I know now is that my parents already knew who they were. They had already gone through the things I was experiencing. They had rebelled against my grandparents; they had felt the emotions I was feeling. But I did not realize it at the time because we were moving at different speeds. I was in high overdrive, moving forward fast in search of something about myself. They had reached their goals, and had already slowed down, cruising.

Comment [29]: Based on the experiences the writer has provided, do you agree with her analysis of her perspective and the change that occurred?

Someday I will be a parent and I will have to teach my child lessons. I hope that my lessons will endure a lifetime. More importantly, I hope my child will learn sooner than I did the value of "walk, don't run."

Comment [30]: Sometimes writers can leave the reader with thoughts to reflect on further. What does the writer leave us to ponder about her life, and how does this question reflect on the reader's own life?

Fiction vs Essays: The Write Way and the Right Way

By Laura Dullum

I had the nightmare again, the one where I know I am asleep, and the essay is due this morning, yet I cannot wake up, so I must compose the essay in my sleep, searching for words, desperately hoping I can remember them when I awake, so I can type it up in time. Those dreams at least help my subconscious mind to generate new ideas. Worse still are the nightmares where the assignment has changed, so I must start over from scratch, trying to read a new textbook and answer a new question, only to awake with the words useless because there is no new essay, only the same old one, and the same old fears. Everyone has heard about people whose stage fright is so severe they throw up if they give an oral report, but how many people get stress stomachaches from essays?

Of course, the essay is not really due this morning; rather, days of work remain. Days of stomachaches, nights of bad dreams, hours and hours of writing and rewriting. My dread is especially ironic, since I have always loved creative writing. Why is my essay-anxiety so intense, when I have always done well and so should have nothing to fear? Why are composition courses so much scarier than literature classes? What part of essay writing triggers my emotional reaction? Logically, there is no reason for me to be so worried, because except for one C and a few B's, I earned A's on every essay I have written. I should feel comfortable with any assignment I could possibly get, but I do not. My past experiences with writing, plus the inherent differences in the nature and purposes of writing fiction vs writing essays, both contribute to my fear of failure.

> **Comment [31]:** What effect do the questions the writer poses have on you as you read the beginning of this essay?

When I think back on my writing experiences, I realize my polarization between fun-fiction and scary-work began very early on. My first memories of writing come from preschool, where I could select from hundreds of stickers, put my choices on a piece of paper, and then a parent volunteer would write down whatever story I made up. I learned to read at age three, and I loved the sticker stories because I felt I was making my own books, just like Dr. Seuss. From my toddler years all through grade school, I was always playing make-believe, Barbie dolls, or dress-up with my

Comment [32]: Notice the way the writer uses her past experience to make her points. In what ways is the writer analyzing while she is reporting on past experiences?

friends, being detectives solving a mystery or princesses battling an evil wizard. To me, those were stories, and I was a storyteller, like the writers whose novels I devoured on a weekly basis.

And yet, I dreaded the physical act of writing. I have always had horrible hand-eye coordination, so physically forming letters was an almost impossible ordeal. I learned to write stories the same way I learned to talk, by reading and by playing, almost by osmosis; I cannot recall a single "how-to-write content" lesson until I learned essay writing my sophomore year in high school. Before that, writing lessons meant penmanship: The tedious, time-consuming process of copying out letters over and over, never my own ideas, my handwriting never matching the sample, always incorrect, never the one right way. Finally, just when I mastered printing, there came cursive, and my ordeal began again, and when cursive finally began to feel natural to me, there came typing, and more pain; my fingers could never seem to keep up with my thoughts. Always, there were writing lessons, and then there was real writing—the kind I did in my mind, or when the teacher had us write stories at home, and I could take my time. It is as if those early experiences colored my attitude by linking essays to penmanship and never being good enough, perhaps because both were formally taught, and unlike creating stories, neither came naturally, but only after a difficult struggle. Maybe this is why I enjoy literature classes, where essays consist of my response to the fiction I love, but I dread composition courses, which involve formal writing lessons I associate with judgment and fear of failure.

After all, as much as I love writing fiction, I long since made a deliberate decision not to take any creative writing courses, because that would require writing for someone else's grade instead of being true to my story. When I write creatively, it is a natural process, like a flower unfolding, so natural that there is no process.

Comment [33]: How do the metaphors the writer uses advance her argument?

Just me, and this living story inside wanting to be born, a need for it to come out into ink, but no outside force. There are no deadlines, so I am free to work on several stories at once, switching between them as inspiration urges. Aside from the many binders full of completed stories, I have literally dozens of journals from high school and college, all filled with ideas, whole scenes sketched out, even half-novels, some on computer, some not, with ideas left to grow and added to months or even years later, a character moved out of one story into another, or two plot lines combined into one.

It is like being a paleontologist of my own mind, digging up bones and putting them together, only to see the horn is actually a claw, or that a piece goes with another body, at once a sense of creating new life and of discovering something that already existed within me. When someone else connects with my writing, I feel wonderful, but I do not require that connection to feel fulfilled, because I write out of my own need. Like a flower, creative writing exists of its own accord; a flower's scent can give joy, but the flower is no less a flower if no one smells it, nor is a flower correct or incorrect; it just is.

With essay writing, there can also be joy, the thrill of realizing what an author is saying in a text and the desire to share my discovery. However, that same desire to explain my ideas is also frightening, because if I cannot explain, then my writing has failed. Where creative writing comes from within, an essay's impetus is imposed from the outside. With writing fiction for myself, I just write, where in an essay, it is not "do it—write," it is "do it right." There is a deadline to meet and a teacher who expects me to fulfill certain standards, standards I cannot fully know until I receive the piece back with its grade. Essay writing is done for someone else and done for a specific purpose: To create a place for public discourse. An essay is like a house, built to invite readers in to hear my ideas, and as host, I want my guests to be pleased with their stay in my home.

Writing an essay, like building a house, is a labor-intensive process. First surveying the site: Reading the book, underlining passages that interest me, and taking notes in the margin about reoccurring imagery, a theme I see, an idea on why the author used a certain word, or any other thoughts. When the teacher actually hands out the assignment, rereading for the specific topic is like making the blueprints, and typing up potential quotes is like putting the walls up brick by brick, with my analysis as mortar. Then the interior decorating: Arranging my ideas like furniture, formalizing a rough draft like painting walls, and of course house-cleaning, when I remove all the clutter, deleting sentences or whole paragraphs, until several pages—and many hours—of work are gone.

This part is hardest of all, because though some deletions are mere clutter, others are favorite phrases or good insights well worthy of inclusion, passages that enrich the essay. It is one thing to

Comment [34]: Here the writer extends a metaphor. In what ways does this clarify her explanation?

turn a weak seven-page essay into a strong six-page essay, and another to make that six-page essay into a five-page essay which is equally strong, yet does not say all I want. In fiction, no limits exist. But essay page requirements, like zoning laws, must be met, and though keeping only the best parts makes my essays stronger, no one likes having to wall off a room in their home. Next comes mopping floors and polishing doorknobs, revisions and more revisions, and all the while the dreaded building inspection looms ever closer—as eager as I am to welcome the guests and show off my new house, there is not just readers' response, but also a grade.

Comment [35]: By the end of the essay, are you finding yourself in agreement with what the writer says? What parts did you find most convincing?

That is what grading is like, a building inspection, and if my house is not up to code—a code I have never seen, and can only guess at—then come the bulldozers. Like faulty wiring, errors can be invisible, until I experience an electric shock. If the house or the essay was structurally unsound, everything may suddenly collapse around me, emotionally as well as metaphorically. Often, a teacher's comments give new insight, and though adding a window to a home is hard work, the rush of light and improved view is worth the effort. Other times, it seems to be a matter of taste, green doors instead of blue, one phrase and not another, and though green may look better, I liked blue more.

Perhaps this is what makes essay writing so difficult for me, the problem of balancing my own vision with my desire to please professors. I am not writing purely for myself as with fiction, but rather for people I know, whose opinions I value, and who I will be seeing in class, having to face them knowing I disappointed them. With contests, I do not feel like a failure if I do not win, perhaps because contests do not give back any criticism, so I never learn if someone thought my carefully crafted metaphor was dull or too ornate—there, no one tells me that my write-way is not the right way. Yet in contests, I never learn how to improve my writing, and the whole point of essay writing is to learn, not just about the topic or my opinion of it, but also about writing itself. And by learning what causes my fear of essay writing, in time, I may learn to overcome it.

Freewriting: Its Uses and Applications in Academic Essays

By Laura Dullum

As a writer, I enjoy doing creative writing on my own, yet I experience anxiety over academic essay assignments. In "Fiction vs Essays," I examined how my different feelings towards writing fiction and writing essays stem from two main sources. First, writing fiction for myself creates a sense of freedom and individuality, because I can choose whatever topic I wish and can write in any style, while essays are usually on assigned topics and have strict rules about format, length, and other stylistic conventions, which can create a sense of oppression that makes writing seem forced and stilted. Secondly, when writing fiction I seek only to please myself and be true to the story, while essays are graded for credit, which creates a fear of failure. Because of these feelings, I often dreaded composition courses, but I've discovered that one of composition courses' chief teaching methods, freewriting, actually resembles creative writing more than an academic essay. Through the use of freewriting, I discovered how to develop a formal essay with less fear, but first I had to learn to really freewrite, instead of constantly stopping to edit.

Freewriting seems to be a widespread teaching method, and all the sources I found supported it, though with some reservations. Many of the contributors to *Nothing Begins With N*, as well as Peter Elbow and several other scholars whose essays I read, use daily freewriting in their classes or in their own writing process. *Nothing Begins With N*, a book containing sixteen essays on freewriting, defines freewriting by its lack of constraints: There is no assigned topic and no grade, no requirement to use correct spelling or standardized grammar, no audience unless the writer chooses to share it, and no insistence that it be "good"—or even comprehensible—writing (xii). In fact, the only rule is that the writer keeps writing without stopping and without doing any editing.

Comment [36]: At this point in the essay, the writer makes her first textual reference. Based on what she says at this point, how do you expect she will be using texts and how does this affect your reading?

Peter Elbow, one of the teachers who originated the use of freewriting, feels "freewriting may be what I care most about in writing . . . I learn [the] most from it. I get my best ideas and writing from it. I get my best group and community work done that way. I feel most myself when I freewrite. I think freewriting helps my students more than anything else . . . and they usually agree . . . I get the same response from teachers" (*Everyone*, 113). Elbow's description captures what freewriting advocates see as freewriting's key traits: It promotes learning, provides a means for writers to tap into their ideas, aids peer collaboration, and fosters individualism through self-discovery.

Comment [37]: What is the relationship between this quote by Robert Whitney and what follows? Why do you think the writer put the quote at the beginning of the paragraph rather than the end? What would have been the difference had it been at the end?

Robert Whitney notes, "I have found this practice [freewriting] to be especially helpful with . . . writers who edit so obsessively that they suppress all sense of feeling, voice, thought, and even meaning in their writing" because they are "so extremely anxious about 'doing it right' that nothing that ends up on the page has any life to it at all" (219). As a high anxiety writer, I can relate to Whitney's observation. Essay Three, which my professor found to be my best work, grew out of a freewrite about how "with writing fiction for myself, I just write, where in an essay, it is not 'do it - write,' it is 'do it right.'" Similarly, Kristy, a fellow student in my college composition course, says of Essay Four, "I spent the least amount of time" on it compared to the other essays "and it was my best paper because I didn't over-think it." The professor agreed with Kristy's assessment of her paper, copying it for the class to read—interestingly, of the five essays printed, at least two (Kristy's and mine), were our least self-censored work, which suggests the absence of inhibition improves writing.

Another of Robert Whitney's observations that resounded with me was his comment that "the most constrained writers do stop" during freewriting to "edit, crossing out words or phrases and rewriting them," something I frequently found myself doing on this composition course's focused freewriting logs (220). Tellingly, the freewrite which proved most useful, and which grew into Essay Three, was one of the few freewrites where I did not delete, rephrase, or otherwise edit while writing. This reflects Peter Elbow's view that "The problem is . . . editing at the same time you are trying to produce" because "compulsive, premature editing doesn't just make writing hard. It also makes writing dead" (*Writ-*

ing, 5–6). Freewriting provides an antidote to such premature editing not only because freewriting specifically forbids stopping to edit, but also because it suspends grammar rules (one of the main things people edit for). However, freewriting's most potent weapon against premature editing may be that no one else reads it, so there is no future critic who must be pleased. Of the two types of freewriting in this class, both logs and essay preliminaries count as part of the course grade. Tellingly, I did the most editing on the logs, since I thought of them as final versions of an assignment, which meant they had to be perfect. In contrast, it was much easier for me to keep writing without stopping to edit on the preliminaries, because I thought of them as preparation for the essay, with the final essay—not its drafts—as what would be graded. The freewriting which grew into "Fiction vs Essays" was a preliminary, not a log, which contributed to it being one of my least constrained, least edited freewrites.

Comment [38]: The writer is referring to a particular experience in her writing class. Were you able to follow her point or would you have liked more information to make the experience clear? How do you think this would be read by someone who is not in a writing class or writing the assignments of the class?

In "Teaching Writing in the Age of Narcissism," William Wright, Jr., notes that freewriting can be "a powerful act of discovery" whose "importance . . . lies not only in its idea-gathering potential but also in its potential as a means of understanding the self" (29). However, as his title suggests, his support of freewriting's ability to generate ideas is leavened by a concern freewriting's emphasis on individualism may endanger its usefulness in an academic environment. Wright cautions against letting freewriting become "a sort of 'feelie-weelie' phenomenon" which provides emotional benefits but has no wider academic application (29). To counter this risk, Wright emphasizes that "prewriting must, of course, be revised and crafted into a finished piece" (29).

Similarly, Kathi McClure notes, "Freewriting and other brainstorming strategies are the beginning of process, not its sum total" (947). Elbow agrees, "Editing [is] crucial, but it is only the last step" (*Writing*, 38). Though McClure approves of freewriting, she sees it "essentially [as] a way of bringing into consciousness a range of approaches to the writing task at hand," approaches "which are then to be refined in rewriting" (948). McClure emphasizes the final product, implying that freewriting exists to generate ideas for formal papers, and like Wright, she places importance on editing. Teacher Kim Stover, who studied under freewriting founder Ken Macrorie, describes "consciously re-viewing my initially unconscious eruption," and stresses the close connection between freewriting and revising (61). Stover notes, "Freewriting uncovered buried images and allowed new ones; editing got rid of the fat. One without the other is about as useful as one chopstick," and both are of equal importance (61). Stover feels this two-part process, that of freewriting and then revising, results in "students [who] wrote papers without fear" because "the initial freewritings were innocuous— 'it's just freewriting'—: [and] the rewritings removed the writers one step— 'it's just editing'" (62).

Similarly, in the log analyzing "Fiction vs Essays," I observed how "the parts of my essay that flowed easiest" were writing and then editing the freewritten sections, "perhaps because I wrote them as brainstorming only," while "I got bogged down [in] the conclusion, which had to be written from scratch with the knowledge that it would be graded."

Comment [39]: This paragraph has many quotes from the authors of several different texts. How does the writer of this essay help the reader to follow the connections among these quotes? If there are moments in the paragraph that you lose the connection, why do you think it happens and what might the writer have done to help out the reader?

In "Make Freewriting More Productive," Mark Reynolds specifically addresses ways in which freewriting can be polished to produce a formal essay. One of Reynolds' tips, that a writer "see if you have discovered any metaphors for your subject which might provide a different perspective," especially draws on creative writing methods (82). Usually, metaphors are associated with fiction or poetry, not with academic writing, which tends to prefer concrete examples over imaginative imagery. Another of Reynolds' suggestions is that writers "consider the five senses in relation to your freewriting," which is also more of a fiction technique, since academic writing hardly ever includes sensory description (81). This shows how freewriting can be closer to fiction than to academic writing. However, other tips are extremely analytical, as when Reynolds suggests a writer "examine the tenses of your verbs" because this "can indicate a focus on the past, present or future [that] may give direction to further thinking" (82).

Reynolds also recommends that freewriting be used in combination with other prewriting techniques, such as making a "cluster diagram" or "tree diagram" of a freewritten piece, proto-outlining by making lists of different ideas or main points, or applying who-what-when-where-why-how questions to the freewritten text (81). Reynolds also advises writers to look for "the argument or thesis of your freewriting" and then write down "what additional details are needed to support your thesis" (81). In this case, what began as a freewrite ends up as an academic exercise; instead of writing for the sake—or the joy—of writing, the freewrite becomes an attempt to prove a point.

Interestingly, several of Reynolds' tips on using a freewrite as preparation for a formal academic essay have been developed by other advocates of freewriting. Elbow also recommends creating metaphors (*Writing*, 53). In *Shoptalk For College Writers*, Sheryl Fontaine and Cherryl Smith similarly suggest that writers do a freewrite where they use "metaphoric thinking" because it "shows you [things] about the concept that you might not have otherwise noticed" (41, 93, 149). Likewise, both Reynolds and *Shoptalk* suggest writers try freewriting from different points of view. Fontaine and Smith advise a writer to "identify what points of view emerge . . . then listen to them as if to the distinct voices of individuals [and] write out a conversation among these voices" (41, 92). Similarly, Reynolds suggests writers "freewrite again on the same subject from the view of another person," while writers can prepare "an argumentative or persuasive paper" by "freewriting from several sides of the issue to discover multiple perspectives" (82). Reynolds' article, like the college composition textbook *Shoptalk*, uses freewriting to create essay drafts by having students freewrite for specific prompts.

Many composition scholars seem to view freewriting primarily as a means to an end, and usually, that end is an academic essay written on an assigned topic for a grade, the exact opposite of an unjudged, any-topic freewrite. At times, it seems freewriting serves as a bribe—a "fun" way to make students write. But freewriting also works. My essay "Fiction vs Essays" was made up almost entirely of writing generated by the freewriting methods above, metaphor and perspective. Though Essay Three addressed my writing anxiety, that anxiety has begun to lessen. For the first time, I had written an essay the way I wrote fiction: I wrote without worrying about doing it right or wrong, then went back and revised later, a strategy I've applied to my later essays, including this one. As Elbow observes, shutting off my inner censor also helped shut off my fear, and as Stover notes, revisions became "only editing." Suddenly, an essay was like fiction: Creating initial ideas and crafting them into a final form, instead of feeling pressured to be perfect.

Comment [40]: The writer has cited many other writers in this essay. How does she bring it back to herself and her own ideas in the conclusion? How did this conclusion work for you as a reader? How did this essay extend or change the ideas the author presented in "Fiction vs Essays"?

Works Cited

Bartholomae, David, and Peter Elbow. "Interchanges: Responses to Bartoholomae and Elbow." *College Composition and Communications,* Volume 46.1 (1995): 88–89.

Belanoff, Pat, Peter Elbow, and Sheryl I. Fontaine, eds. *Nothing Begins With N: New Investigations of Freewriting.* Carbondale, IL: Southern Illinois University Press, 1991.

Elbow, Peter. *Everyone Can Write: Essays Towards a Hopeful Theory of Writing and Teaching Writing.* New York: Oxford University Press, 2000.

———. *Writing With Power: Techniques For Mastering the Writing Process.* New York: Oxford University Press, 1981.

———. *Writing Without Teachers.* New York: Oxford University Press, 1973.

Fontaine, Sheryl I., and Cherryl Smith. *Shoptalk for College Writers.* New York: Harcourt Brace College Publishers, 1999.

McClure, Kathi. "A Comment on Allan Bloom, Mike Rose, and Paul Goodman: In Search of a Lost Pedagogical Synthesis." *College English,* 56.8 (1994): 947-948.

Reynolds, Mark. "Freewriting's Origin." *The English Journal,* Volume 73.3 (1984): 81–82.

———. "Staffroom Interchange: Make Freewriting More Productive." *College Composition and Communications,* 39.1 (1988): 81–82.

Stover, Kim. "Riposte: In Defense of Freewriting." *The English Journal,* 77.2 (1988): 61–62.

Whitney, Robert. "Why I Hate to Freewrite." In *Nothing Begins With N: New Investigations of Freewriting.* Eds Pat Belanoff, Peter Elbow, and Sheryl I. Fontaine. Carbondale, IL: Southern Illinois University Press, 1991.

Wright, William W. Jr. "Teaching Writing in the Age of Narcissism." *The English Journal,* 69.8, (1980): 26–29.

CHAPTER
15

Guidelines for Reading and Responding to Writers' Drafts

Reviewing the Writing You've Done So Far

When you have completed a first draft, you have completed the first part of writing an essay. First, you used the exploratory writing activities to examine your thoughts, generate ideas, record and analyze information you gathered, and find a focus for your essay; second, with this focus you drafted an essay that used data you had collected as points of evidence to explain and support the claim you wished to make. Many writers consider this first part of writing to be the most difficult part of essay writing—getting through the initial exploration, planning, and writing a draft. Because you will need to write a draft each time you are assigned essays for this course and others, let's review the process more carefully.

As you read and responded to the first three chapters of this book, you wrote informally, producing reflections; the form or style in which these were written was not particularly important. Rather, the content of what they said mattered most. Writing in this way, you could reflect on and record what you read, information you gathered, and your own understanding of both. Then, after generating a number of these reflections, you used the exploratory writing activities we provided to identify connections among the reflections, locating places where the words and ideas in one might be said to intersect with words and ideas in others. During this process of making connections, you found questions, conflicts, contradictions, and associations suggested to you by your own writing. We asked you to reflect and analyze further, to continue writing and observing your own evolving thoughts as you found points of connection emerging from the information you had gathered so far. And as you did this, we also asked you to move toward seeing a focus in what you were writing and thinking about.

Over time, this process of exploring and focusing, exploring and focusing again, helps move your writing toward a first draft of an analytic, reflective essay that works to convey an explicit claim to the reader. This way of reaching a draft parallels the experience of most writers who contend that they do not know exactly what it is they want to say until they find their ideas developing in their own informal, exploratory writing.

The section of writing that takes place up until the completion of a first draft is sometimes called *prewriting* to indicate that writers create lots of informal fragments, thoughts, and ideas on their way to *drafting* a more coherent, essay-like piece of writing. While the term *prewriting* may serve as a useful reminder of how much informal writing must be done in the course of creating a formal essay, it also falsely suggests that real writing does not begin until you are writing a whole draft. But this exploratory and reflective writing, rather than being a stage *before* the real writing begins, *is* the real writing. Moreover, informal writing that helps the writer to make meaning—to generate, sort, re-sort, and expand ideas—is not confined to this early stage in the larger task of essay writing. It goes on throughout the whole process of writing a formal essay. As you will see as you now revise and develop your draft, by writing and rewriting, reading and rewriting, a writer moves slowly, and often painstakingly, toward an increasingly clearer expression of meaning.

Time to Hear How Others Read Your Draft

Just as the first parts of this writing process have been given names—prewriting and drafting—what follows is referred to as *responding and revising*. So far, one distinctive feature of the exploratory freewriting and the drafting you have done is that you probably did not ask anyone else to read what you were writing. In this first part of writing you could write without caring whether another reader would understand what you wrote. Composing in this way allows you to listen carefully to your own developing ideas as you write toward a draft. And, as your draft emerges from the pieces of writing you have composed, the things that you want to say and that you will want your reader to hear are likely to become clearer to you. Thoughtful, engaged rereading of your own drafts helps you to hear the developing meaning in your writing.

By the time at least part of that meaning becomes clear to you, you may be ready to work together with readers, getting their perspective on what you have written. Ultimately, all college writing is written to be shared with other readers, something that presents another challenge for writers.

No matter how perceptively you read your own drafts, how well you read is necessarily limited by what you know. Writers carry an intimate knowledge of the feelings, thoughts, and experiences that lie behind their words. Gaps or confusions in their writing can be invisible to writers because they unwittingly use this knowledge to fill in the gaps or untangle confusions that another reader, without such knowledge, would see. Since, as we discussed earlier, readers of college essays expect to be able to know exactly where the writer stands, the essay needs to speak for itself, to be clear to another reader who does not have access to the writer's private history and knowledge. So, there is great value in having people other than yourself, people who do not have the inside line, read your draft and share with you how they read it, how well they understand it, what questions they want to ask you about it.

Readers bring their own experience and understanding to bear on what they read. The opportunity to hear how several readers make sense of one's writing allows a writer to view the work from the outside, from the perspective of other readers who may have a variety of ways of reading and responding to the same, developing essay.

Notice that we have used the words *responding* and *reading* rather than *evaluating* or *judging*. In the process of reading your drafts, readers may not be able to keep themselves from saying, "I really liked this part," or "I think this is great"—the kind of response that writers usually feel ready to hear. We do not ask you to refrain from this kind of positive comment since it may encourage your fellow writers to keep going through the sometimes difficult task of expanding and finishing an essay. But we want to caution you that *evaluating* an early draft is premature. At this point the work is not complete, and so it would be unfair to offer any critical evaluation. What the draft is ready for and what will be most useful to the writer are for readers to tell how they understand the draft, to ask questions they have, to tell what seems to them to be the main points the draft is making, and so on.

This kind of response to a first draft is very much like having a conversation with friends. You offer your point of view or tell a story, and then you wait for your friends to respond to what you have said, to the content. In a conversation with friends about what you did over the weekend, you certainly do not expect them to evaluate how you presented your story, or to say, "You should have provided a better conclusion," or "I don't like the way you ordered your sentences." However, you do expect that they might comment on what you said, maybe asking for more information ("Who drove to the party?" "How long were you gone?") or for clarification ("What did she say when you got back?" "You mean he never showed up?") or for a main point ("So what is it you're telling us about that place—is it worth going to or not?"). A first draft, like a conversation, is an opportunity for readers or listeners to respond to what you have said. They might continue the conversation by picking up on a certain comment you made; they might laugh at humorous words or lines, agree or disagree with you, ask for more information, or add some of their own. This kind of response allows you to continue the conversation, to fill in information that seems to be needed, or simply to know which of your words got through; it allows you to hear back how someone outside yourself understands what you have said.

Suggestions for Getting Useful Feedback to Your Draft

In conversation, if a friend says that she did not understand something you said, you usually do not abandon the whole idea you were trying to express. More likely you will pause and reconsider what you have said, and perhaps rephrase your idea or elaborate to make it more understandable for your friend. Similarly, readers' responses of the kind we are outlining here are not evaluations of your work but are simply that: readers' responses. As the writer, you have the opportunity to develop your own writing as you choose. The more you can learn about how different readers understand what you have said, the more confidence you can feel about the choices you make as you revise. Often readers' responses are useful to writers in surprising ways; sometimes they can help you to resee what had already seemed to be quite clear and thought out, or help you to view your work in a new way. When you have the opportunity for readers to read your work in progress, knowing that you are not being judged but are being listened to, see if you can take in as much response to your work as you can. And after your readers have run out of things to say, you can ask for response to specific aspects of your draft that you have questions about or you want to do more work on.

Your goal is to listen attentively and openly, without interrupting your readers to defend your draft or to explain what you meant. If you do not help them out or immediately answer questions for them, you are likely to find out more about the possible interpretations of your words on the page. We also suggest that you read your work aloud to readers when you have the opportunity to do so. You will notice that you hear your own words differently when you read them aloud and you may want to make some notes on ideas that occur to you for revisions as you read.

The Role of Readers

Up to this point, the predominant focus of attention in *Writing Your Way Through College* has been on composing college writing. But without readers of these texts, college writing cannot really exist. As you continue on in college, you will become more and more knowledgeable about and comfortable with academic conventions and expectations by being both an academic writer and an academic reader. College writing looks and sounds like it does, in large part, because there are readers who expect it to look and sound this way.

Sometimes, students who are new to college writing feel tongue-tied when their instructors ask them to read and respond to one another's essay drafts. These same students may also be surprised by how much response their instructors can provide to these same drafts. A significant difference between the students and the instructors is that instructors have spent a great deal of time becoming familiar with and internalizing the language and conventions of the academic culture and, in the course of reading countless essays, have also fine-tuned their own response to writing. So, in addition to becoming a better college writer, by participating in the response activities that we outline in the book, you will be serving an apprenticeship in becoming an academic reader.

Although all of us are used to responding to and interacting with each other's spoken language, most people do not have experience responding, in nonjudgmental ways, to writing. When you respond tell *how* you read the draft; ask the questions you really have; give the writer as clear a picture as you can of what you understand and connect to in the text. When it is your turn to read and respond to a classmate's work, your goal is to try to articulate what you heard or read, to describe the understanding you really have. What are your questions? What strikes you about the text? What do you want to know more about?

As you gain experience as a reader of drafts, you are growing as a writer, perhaps as much as you are when you are composing. While it is true that the response you provide to fellow writers will help them to revise, becoming a careful reader of a draft is immediately useful to your own growth as a writer. For, while we can never truly disassociate ourselves from our own texts, a considerable part of the revision process is the work of attempting to see our writing as readers do, to see what readers may need to know, what further information or evidence they may need. By reading others' drafts, we learn how to see our own evolving texts from a reader's point of view.

Making Use of Readers' Responses

Because our individual experiences, affinities, knowledge, and interests come into play as we read any text, it is particularly useful to have the opportunity for several different readers to respond to your draft. Your readers are there to provide response rather than advice on or evaluation of your work, and from these responses you, as the writer, can return to your draft with a broader understanding of how different readers make sense of and react to what you have written. Some readers may have questions to which you wish to respond as you revise. Others may be confused by something in your draft, and this information may affect your next draft. Readers may point out sections of the essay that they were especially drawn in by or that they found particularly intriguing, and this information may also help you as you continue working. If someone disagrees with your argument, you may become aware that there are some points that you have not yet said, or that the order of your comments has been confusing or misleading. You may find that your argument is convincing for some readers and not for others, and this may help you direct the way you address your audience as you revise. Readers' comments may influence what you decide to expand on and what you decide needs to be deleted, the order in which you structure your essay, and what details you wish to include.

Because, as we have said, getting the response of readers to your work as it is evolving is such an important part of the process of writing, in this chapter we have included two sets of guidelines: sources from whom you might receive response to your writing and strategies for reading and telling writers about their drafts. You can follow these guidelines each time your instructor asks you to read and respond to other writers' drafts.

Who Can Read and Respond to Your Drafts?

The more readings of your drafts you can get, the more useful information you will have about how different readers perceive what you have written so far. This information can help as you are revising your essay by giving you a picture of what readers may need in order to see your points more clearly. While you may not have the opportunity to use all of the sources we describe here for every essay, over the course of the semester, it is a good idea to become familiar with the advantages of using each of them.

Response from One Other Person in Class or Online

One excellent source of response to a draft is the intensely focused response of a single individual, someone in your class who is also drafting an essay. The two of you will be familiar with the context in which the essay is being written and with *Writing Your Way Through College* as well as with any particular ways that your instructor is using this text or adapting the assignment. At the same time, you will each be able to concentrate on reading only each other's draft and providing a full and unhurried response.

The particular individual with whom you exchange drafts could vary as the term progresses. This change in readers will provide you with equally varied responses. Sometimes you might want to work with a friend who knows you and your writing style and can, therefore, make some assumptions based on this familiarity; sometimes it can be helpful to work with someone you know only in the context of class and who has no additional information about you, who must rely solely on the draft.

In-Class or Online Response in Groups of Three to Five Students

Your instructor may ask you to form groups that remain a permanent part of your class for the entire term. Or you may form new groups several times during the term. It is also possible to form new groups for each essay. Often, when groups last for several weeks or months, the individuals in the groups find they become used to working together in ways that help their ability to read and respond to each other's writing. However, because the ways of responding about drafts that we describe are nonjudgmental, but simply reveal how your words make readers think, you should not feel apprehensive, even with a new group of readers. This is a positive way to learn about other people's experiences and ideas and to communicate your own ideas and experiences to others.

You may decide to divide up the response strategies among the members of the group so that each draft is assured of getting all the different forms of response, or you may just let the response evolve more spontaneously. If you are working in class and not online, it is a good idea for readers to write down their responses or to allow time for the writer to make some notes to help him or her remember the responses.

Response from Someone Outside of Class

Individuals who are not directly connected to your writing class can give you a clear sense of how your draft is working on its own. They can offer response that tells you whether or not the draft, so far, can be read and understood without the special information available to students enrolled in your class who are writing the same assignment.

Response from Your School's Writing Center

If your school has a writing center, take your draft to a tutor for response. Tutors have experience with reading student writing and can provide you with useful feedback to your draft. You may want to have some questions in mind for the tutor, something that will help to focus your discussion of the essay.

Using the Strategies for Reading and Responding to Drafts

The four strategies we include here will help you to read a draft (your own or someone else's) and then to articulate into a response your understanding of what you read in ways that help the writer to see the draft from a reader's perspective. We have arranged these reading and response strategies in the order that you may want to use them, progressing from a first reading, to later, more studied readings. As your essay evolves, it is useful to get additional feedback from the same or different readers.

Once you and your readers become comfortable using these strategies, you will be able to read and respond to each other's work quite spontaneously, probably without referring much to this outline. For now, try out each strategy to get used to the way it works.

Strategies for Reading and Responding

1. Holistic Reading and Responding

On your first reading (or hearing) of a draft, read to get a general impression, to find out what the main focus seems to be, and to discover the main points the writer is making. On this first reading, you will not be expected to formulate a detailed response, so simply give your full attention to the text. This form of reading is critical to all the other forms; it is the foundation for your ability to be a helpful responder. From a holistic reading you can provide the kind of first response that writers need: to know that someone is really listening and taking in what they have written.

Once you have finished reading, make a list for the writer that completes the following phrases:

1. So far, I understand your focus to be . . .

2. Some main points I noticed were . . .

3. Some lines or phrases that most caught my attention were . . .

2. Narrative Reading and Responding

Another way of reading is to pay attention to your own process of reading the text. You cannot know with certainty exactly what the writer intended to say, but you are an authority on your own reading. The idea is to focus on what happens to you and in you as you read, to chronicle the story of what goes through your mind. The story of your own reading is not a summary or an analysis; it is a narrative of the thoughts, ideas, feelings you had at specific points as you read or heard the draft.

After this reading, use these phrases to begin the responses you provide the writer:

1. Here is a place where I felt I understood the focus of the essay . . .

2. Here is a place where I wanted to know more . . .

3. At this point I expected the text to say . . .

4. I got especially interested at the point that . . .

5. At this point I had a question . . .

6. The evidence that was most convincing is . . .

7. I was not sure of the connection to the rest of the essay in the part where . . .

8. At this point I thought some other evidence might be . . .

9. Here I thought of something that contradicted the text . . .

3. Analytic Reading and Responding

You are probably more familiar with analytical readings of drafts than with any of the other kinds of readings. Here, you are reading to see how the writer seems to be building his or her argument, interpreting the evidence, and accomplishing his or her goals for the essay.

Since the essay is not yet finished, writers can use readers' analytical readings to help them think about what more they may want to add to the essay, how they may want to restructure specific sections, and so on. Use these phrases to guide the response once you have read analytically:

1. The goals for the draft seem to be . . .

2. These goals are accomplished in these ways . . .

3. The main points seem to be . . .

4. The evidence for these points is . . .

4. Collaborative Reading and Responding

In collaborative reading, the reader and writer discuss the content, structure, and style of the draft, devise plans for revising, and come up with possible supporting evidence or further ideas. In this kind of reading, the reader acts like a collaborator or coauthor of the draft, going beyond a description of his or her reading or of the text and actually brainstorming with the writer about places in the draft that may need elaboration or more focus. Of course, the writer of the draft is the first author in the collaboration; the writer benefits from the opportunity for several collaborations to draw upon as he or she determines how to revise.

During a collaborative reading, use the following questions to focus your response for all of the essays in this book. Additional questions follow for the particular essays you will write.

1. Are there sections that seem incomplete?

2. What further evidence could be added?

3. What could be added for clarification?

4. What might be a good title for the essay?

Additional Questions for Collaborative Response

For Essays 1 and 2, Based on Information from Observing and Listening

As a final way of reviewing a draft, readers can focus on the way that evidence is used and analyzed in the draft so far. The following questions are specific to using information from observing and listening to what people say. Keeping the intended focus of the draft in mind, answer these questions about your own draft and gather answers to these questions from a reader:

1. How does the draft use information gathered from conversation and observation to support or develop the focus or main claim of the essay? How does the draft limit the extent of the conclusions drawn from the information?

2. What points or observations are made in the draft based on the writer's understanding or interpretation of the conversations and interviews he or she has gathered? What makes them convincing? Is there anything that does not seem convincing?

3. Where in the essay are conversations paraphrased and/or directly quoted? What seems to be the purpose for which each quotation or paraphrase is included? Are any of the passages longer than needed? Are any of them incomplete?

4. How does this draft interpret, for the reader, what others have said? How does it use the words or actions of someone else to illustrate or extend the points being made in the essay? Is the interpretation or explanation incomplete or unclear in any places?

5. What does the writer do in the essay to make the information seem credible and authoritative? How does the writer make clear who the source is and why this source would be appropriate and convincing in relation to the claim or meaning of the essay?

For Essays 3 and 4, Based on Information from Recollections and Memories

The ways of responding we have listed earlier can be applied to any draft. Some additional response, specific to the kind of information you have incorporated into your essay, can also be helpful. One of the lessons you'll learn as you write college essays is how to use most convincingly, effectively, and appropriately the kind of information available to you. Before answering the following questions, remind yourself of what you take to be the essay's explicit claim or meaning. Keeping the focus and claim of the draft in mind, answer these questions about your own draft and gather answers to these questions from a reader.

1. How are instances of recollection and memory used in relation to the main claim of the essay?

2. What points or observations does this draft make based on this information? What makes these points convincing? Are there any that are not convincing?

3. Where do recollection and memory appear in the essay? What seems to be the purpose for which each instance of recollection or memory is presented? Are there further details that could be included? Are there some details that do not seem to connect to the essay?

4. How are the recollections cited? Is there more you would like to know about the context of the recollections, about when and where the event took place?

For Essays 5 and 6, Based on Information Gathered from Written Texts

The following are some questions responding readers might ask to help you think about how you have used information from written texts, the information source for these essays. Before answering these questions, responders should remind themselves of what they found to be the essay's explicit claim or meaning. Keeping that clearly in mind, answer these questions to give the writer your sense of how he or she used the information in this draft.

1. How does the writer use information from written texts to support or develop the essay? To what extent are the specific references to written texts an integral part of the essay? That is, how do the references advance the explicit meaning of the essay and help to establish the authority of the writer? Are there other references that might be added? Are the references that are included commented upon and explained in the essay?

2. What particular points or observations does the writer make based on his or her interpretation or understanding of the texts that are cited? Tell the writer what makes these points convincing for you. Tell the writer any that feel to you unconvincing. What would make them more convincing?

3. In what ways are references to written texts being made: Quotations? Paraphrases? Summaries? In what ways do these seem to be effective

choices or not? If whole passages are cited, how does the writer make use of these, and do they seem to be valuable, as they stand, to the essay?

4. How do the references to written texts fit into content of the essay? Is there more you would like to know about how the writer is interpreting or understanding any particular citation or about its original source?

CHAPTER 16

Guidelines for Editing
Final Revisions

Reading Your Penultimate Draft for Surface Presentation

While you have been drafting and revising your essay, we have been encouraging you to focus on the meaning and purpose you are developing rather than on the way you are presenting your ideas. When writers turn to editorial and proofreading concerns too soon, focusing on spelling or punctuation or word usage, they can easily lose track of their thoughts. Giving over attention to word choice or syntax or spelling rather than to the ideas he or she is on the verge of making and finding, a writer may even block his or her own ability to write. But once the writer has revised to the point that the ideas are expressed in ways readers can understand, then attention to usage or format or spelling is not only appropriate but necessary.

Although your ideas have been the main focus of your drafting process so far, at the same time, you have been making choices about what words to use, the order of your sentences and paragraphs, and so on. Your attention to meaning, however, has kept you from debating over surface-level concerns like individual word order and punctuation choices and correct spelling. Having gone through the work of the previous chapters, at this point you can take time to focus on these secondary concerns and on the overall presentation of your essay.

As we discussed earlier, the nature of the language used in college is in flux, and what constitutes standardized English is evolving, but academic readers who read college essays do have expectations that you can meet by reviewing the surface presentation of your essay. For when your essay doesn't meet these expectations, it may not be read as seriously as it might otherwise. If a word is misspelled, for instance, readers may still be able to understand the intended meaning. However, academic readers—and you, yourself, are now becoming an academic reader—expect words to be spelled correctly in college writing, and they notice when they are not. Readers take their attention away from the ideas in the text and, however briefly, focus attention on the misspelled word. We believe that when readers do this, your essay may not be getting as good a reading as it would otherwise, without the reader's shift of attention.

Spelling is a particularly easy surface feature to address since it is one of the few editing concerns that has only one right answer. That is, since English spelling was standardized in the eighteenth century, there is only one way (or a preferred and a second way!) for any word in English to be spelled. Although we recommend that you compose your draft with, or at some stage enter the draft into, a computer using a program that has a spell checker, you will not always be able to rely on someone else, or technology, even for decisions about spelling. Your spell checker will not recognize some words and will not correct for words that are misused.

Along with spelling, there are several other surface features that seem to disturb academic readers, to take their attention away briefly from the meaning of your text. These are not necessarily the most important surface features, and for some readers other constructions may be more distracting.

To ensure that your ideas are taken seriously and are as available as possible to academic readers, it is useful to be familiar with which usage and textual features are most likely to disrupt your readers' attention from the meaning of your essay, and what strategies you can apply to edit and proofread for these concerns. What follows is a discussion of potential distractions for academic readers and some suggestions for helping writers make choices about editing and proofreading in light of how academics read student texts. We have provided a check list of readers' distractions on pages 151–52. We have also included some distractions that are specific to the particular sources of writing you will use in each essay. It is important that you examine these for each essay you write. Be sure to look back at these descriptions should you need a reminder.

Usage Distractions for Academic Readers and Suggestions for Writers

Most sentence-level distractions would not be noticed at all, or would not disturb most academics, if they occurred in speech rather than in writing. Indeed, the first six distractions we describe are silent in speech, even if you are reading aloud from a written text. Following these, we give a brief description of the audible distractions (7–9) that might hinder your readers' progress through your essay. It is our experience that although there are other editing issues, a college writer who learns to correct for these nine distractions will appear to be writing standard enough English to receive a good reading, that is, a reading as good as anyone one else might receive from an academic reader. Your instructor may suggest you buy a handbook to supplement your dictionary as a resource for the many other usage issues that occur in conventional Standard English.

Silent Distractions

1. Spelling

Academic *readers* often make severe judgments about writers' abilities based on the correctness of their spelling. It is common for readers to assume that an inordinate number of misspellings indicates laziness or irresponsibility in the writer. The assumption that writers just don't care is especially strong when they misspell common words (for example, *suppose to* instead of *supposed to*; *there* when it should be *their* or *they're*; *it's* when it should be *its*) or make common errors, ones that readers have seen so many times that they become pet peeves or annoyances. *Writers* can correct spelling errors using a spell checker on the computer or a good dictionary. In fact, because spell checkers can't identify homonyms (a spell checker will find that *threw* is spelled correctly even if you really meant to use *through*) or misplaced words (She it the one who threw it), it is important to have a dictionary on hand too.

Some people who have good visual memories are adept at spelling. Others, including many famous writers, need to look up words before letting a piece of writing stand on its own. If spelling is not particularly easy for you, you will need to take time to look up longer or uncommon words in a dictionary.

2. Typos

Like spelling errors, typos may be used by *readers* to make a quick determination of your skill and the commitment you have to your writing. *Writers* can locate some typos using a spell checker; others will get by since they may be correctly spelled words, but not the words you intended. One useful strategy for seeing typos is to read your essay from the end, moving word by word backward through the text. This process can help highlight the typos for you. Final versions of essays need to be proofread for typing mistakes. If you notice a mistake just as you are turning in a final version of a paper, it is always better to correct it than to have a perfectly neat paper.

3. Capitalization

Capitalization has virtually no effect on the *reader's* understanding of a text, but a misplaced capital, or a missing one, sends a distress signal to an academic reader that may take her attention away from your essay. Because capitalization errors are often the result of a typing mistake, it is important for *writers* to check that words that need capitals, like names of people or places and first words of sentences, are capitalized and that words that don't need capitals are not capitalized. Reading the essay backward word by word is often a useful strategy for finding missing capitalizations too.

4. Formatting

Like spelling, typos, and capitalization, formatting has no effect on meaning. However, academic *readers* expect paragraph indentations and will be disturbed if your whole essay appears in one paragraph. It is a matter of the *writer's* choice where to break paragraphs. Two-page and single-sentence paragraphs are unusual but are not incorrect. The general wisdom about paragraphing is that when you move on, in some way or degree, to a new topic, it is time for a new paragraph. Reread any chapter of this text (or any other academic text) to get a sense of paragraphing.

Other usual formatting issues in the U.S. are that most academic papers are double spaced, typed, have standard one-inch margins, use average-size font, and are presented on standard weight, white, 8½-by-11-inch paper. Academic papers are expected to look alike.

5. Possessives

We have listed possessives under silent distractions because the proofreading concern we want to highlight regarding possessives is the apostrophe ('). Whether or not we hear, in speech, the *s* signifying the possessive in *the boy's bike* or *the boys' bikes*, in college writing, *readers* expect the apostrophe to appear, standing for "belongs to." While checking for possessives, the *writer* should look for missing instances as well as for any apostrophes that appear in the text unnecessarily. Apostrophes are used only in forming contractions (like *can't* and *wouldn't*) and for possessives. No apostrophe should appear where a plural is intended except if it is a plural possessive.

6. Sentence Boundaries

When we speak it is often not possible and it is certainly not necessary to identify where one sentence ends and the next begins. Like the first four distractions, sentence boundaries are of concern only to *readers*, not to listeners. Sentence boundaries seem to matter a great deal to academic readers even though, like the other silent distractions, they usually have no effect on one's ability to understand a text. In editing one's own essay, the *writer* should know that there are only two possible inconsistencies in the category of sentence boundaries: (1) fragments, in which you write part of a sentence but punctuate it as if it is a complete sentence, and (2) fused or run-on sentences, in which you write two sentences together but punctuate as if you have written one sentence. Under certain circumstances—for emphasis—fragments are acceptable, though usually student writing is expected to be free of fragments; fused and run-on sentences are not acceptable in college writing, although long, correctly punctuated sentences are sometimes valued as part of a particularly academic style.

We know of no fully reliable rule for what makes a complete sentence in English. The general formula is that one needs a subject and a predicate, the person or thing the sentence is about and a description of that subject's action or state of being. "He stands" is a complete sentence, but "Standing idly by the streetlight, the sirens blaring, the horns honking" is not a complete sentence because there is no subject; you're left to say, "Who is standing idly . . . ?" "The quiet, long-haired boy in the front of the line" is also an incomplete sentence because there is no predicate. You're left to say, "What about the quiet, long-haired boy?" Our favorite test for complete sentences is to imagine that the sentence is all someone said when he walked into the room; would the sentence make some kind of complete sense, or would you ask the kind of questions the fragments in the previous examples provoke?

It is difficult to notice fragments because they are usually made complete by attaching them to the previous or following sentence. So, when you are writing, you make that connection in your mind. If you have two complete sentences you can either divide them up with a period (.) or you can join them together with a semicolon (;) or with a conjunction such as *and*, *or*, or *but*. You can't join two sentences together with a comma (,). The best technique we know of for checking sentence boundaries is to read a paper, sentence by sentence, backward. If you start with the last sentence of the essay, then read the next to last, and so on, you will be able to focus on sentence completeness without being influenced by the meaning of the text.

Audible Distractions

7. Agreement

The meaning of a sentence is rarely affected by the convention of agreement, but nonstandard agreement is a particularly powerful distraction for academic *readers*. Agreement means that there is consistency within a sentence. The main parts of the sentence are either both plural or both singular. The form of the verb depends on whether the sentence contains a singular or plural subject. In the same way, singular or plural pronouns match singular or plural antecedents. To meet the expectations of academic readers, you will need to check for both subject-verb agreement and pronoun-antecedent agreement.

Using a handbook is often a useful way for *writers* to check for agreement. In general, you will need to review each sentence first to see that the form of the verb matches that of the subject: In the sentence "Each student has a notebook," the singular subject *student* matches the verb form *has*. In the sentence "Students take tests in chemistry," the plural subject *students* matches the verb form *take*. Second, you will need to see that in a sentence the antecedent, which is the word a pronoun refers to, is plural if the pronoun is plural and singular if the pronoun is singular. In the sentence "Musicians must practice if they want to become accomplished performers," the plural pronoun *they* matches the plural antecedents *musicians* and *performers*. In the sentence "A musician must practice if he or she wants to become an accomplished performer," the singular pronouns *he* and *she* match the singular antecedents *musician* and *performer*. Again, agreement is a convention of standard college writing that you can give attention to at the point when you are making the presentation of your essay conform to the expectations of academic readers.

8. Tense

The academic *reader* who encounters a surprising, nonstandard tense shift in a college essay will, as with the other audible distractions, still be able to understand what is being said. He or she may pause to reflect on the writer's language history or background, surmising that this is a speaker of other languages besides English or other dialects besides the standard one. Even if the writer's background or history is the subject of the essay, the academic reader will expect the writer's knowledge of other languages and dialects to remain invisible in the finished text. (We believe that, at this time, the academic world is biased in favor of the standard form, although this bias is undergoing debate and change.)

In editing and proofreading, the *writer* will want to focus, again, on the verbs in the sentences, perhaps using the handbook to help. Are the verbs in their standard form? Is the tense consistent within sentences or paragraphs, and, when there is a tense change, does it make sense in the context of the rest of the paragraph or essay?

9. Word Choice

The final audible distraction is word choice, or diction. Academic *readers* find acceptable a wide range of language and diction. But they expect words to be used in conventional ways. As a *writer*, you may want to review your draft for the accuracy and appropriateness of the words, something that is not always easy to distinguish. We advise you to choose words from your own vocabulary, which is enormous, rather than use a thesaurus to find unfamiliar words that you may not be able to use conventionally. We also encourage you to ask others if you are unsure of the choice you have made; be sure to ask for their explanation, not just their decision. Word choice options include not only replacing words that are used incorrectly but finding the most precise words to express your ideas and reach your audience.

Additional Advice for Editing and Proofreading

In addition to the particular strategies we have mentioned already, we find that it is always helpful to read your draft aloud, slowly, paying attention to agreement, tenses, and word choice. And finally, because the distractions we identified may or may not be immediately visible to you in your draft, it is advisable to get some help in locating points where some changes in the draft may be warranted. As we suggested, all of the distractions call for decisions to be made by the writer. While some distractions, like spelling and formatting, may present only one option for the writer, most editorial concerns can be resolved in a variety of ways. When you are editing and proofreading someone else's text, do not make any changes on the draft. Your job will be to locate any places where you feel there may be distractions, about which the writer will then make an editorial decision. The key here is not to correct one another's essays, but to identify places where the writer may want to consider editing. Discuss the places you marked in each other's essays. If possible, exchange with someone else in class so that you have more than one other reader's review.

All of the distractions for academic readers that we have listed force a cautionary stance on writers that is in direct opposition to the open stance of generating writing. That is why it is important to treat the distractions as the most superficial part of writing. Nevertheless, you may find that focusing on the surface features of the text will allow you to fine-tune your presentation in ways that make your meaning even more available to readers.

A Checklist for Editing

The following is a checklist or overview of the guidelines for editing. Your instructor may ask you to use all or some of these as you work with one another's drafts. At the end of the overview, we have added some additional distractions that are specific to each source of writing assigned in this book.

Silent Distractions

spelling

typos

capitalization

formatting

possessives

sentence boundaries

> *Audible Distractions*
> agreement
> tense
> word choice
>
> *Additional Distractions*
> citing each source of information

Additional Editing Concerns for Essays Informed by Observing and Listening

In writing essays whose source is conversations and observations, as with all college writing, to be honest and establish the authority of your information, it is necessary that you cite your information and do so conventionally. As you read the examples that follow, be sure to notice the use of quotation marks and the placement of punctuation. If you are unsure about this, refer to your handbook.

You can include what someone said by using a direct quotation, an exact replication of what was originally said. The person who stated the words can be identified at the beginning, end, or middle of the quote. For example, inserting the speaker's identity into the middle of the quote, you might write:

> "The first time I used my pager," explained my friend Nancy, "I had no idea what some of the codes meant or how to find out their meaning."

And, if appropriate, the source of the reference—where or when it was initially spoken—is also included:

> Speaking at a school town meeting, Mr. Jones argued, "If our children are to become better readers and writers, we need to be willing to pay for smaller class size and better teachers" (October 2005).

You can also convey what someone said less exactly using an indirect quote or a paraphrase; these are instances in which the writer rephrases, in his or her own words and in a structure appropriate to the essay he or she is writing, the words of someone else. As in a direct quote, however, the source of the information is included. This can be incorporated into the body of the essay. For instance, an essay might include an indirect quote of Mr. Jones' comment about schools:

Improving children's reading and writing skills is not something that can be done without expense to taxpayers. Mr. Jones, the local school principal, has argued to parents at the October school board meeting that the single best way to improve reading scores and help children write better is to reduce the number of students in each class. This, of course, would mean that more teachers would have to be hired and paid for their work.

Additional Editing Concerns for Essays Informed by Recollections and Memory

Whatever their explicit purpose or meaning, these essays have been developed from and supported by information from your personal recollections and memories. Sometimes, in order to make this information more authoritative and credible or because it would be dishonest not to, writers cite their sources. They might include a direct naming of their source within the body of their writing or an internal reference to an actual date or a place. For example, you might find it necessary to indicate the original source of your own words or phrases: "How many times have I said to my own friends the words that my dad used to repeat to me, 'The squeaky wheel gets the grease'?" Or you might need to cite something you yourself wrote in the past: "In writing the 'Farewell to the Counselors' speech (Camp Trefoil, August 2005), I found myself surprisingly able to find words that never would have come to me had I been writing for school."

Keep in mind that the purpose of citations is to indicate what words or ideas you have borrowed or built on (even if the first ones were your own) and to establish your own authority as someone who understands the value of knowledge and information that is passed on from person to person or place to place.

Additional Editing Concerns for Essays Informed by Written Texts

When writing essays whose source of purpose and support is written texts, you are expected to cite your sources of information according to the conventions of standard American college English. The main concern here is that you honestly and correctly identify words and ideas from other people's texts, whether these texts originally appeared in a journal, a book, a newspaper, or on the computer screen.

In American culture, ideas are treated like property, as if they were owned by the person who uttered or wrote them. Consequently, not identifying the owner is comparable to stealing someone else's property, an act that is called *plagiarism*. When your sources are not cited in the conventional way, your instructor may assume that you don't understand the concept of plagiarism and simply ask you to rewrite your essay. However, sometimes instructors will feel quite strongly that even though you do not know the formal conventions for citing written sources, you are still responsible for the citations you use. In this case, the penalty for plagiarism can be quite severe—ranging from a failing grade on an essay or in a course to suspension or expulsion from school.

But the process of identifying written sources and the formal conventions for making such citations are no more difficult than they were when you identified sources for other kinds of information. In the essays you have already completed, when your information sources were recollection and memory of personal experiences or observations and conversations, you identified the experiences or events and the people with whom you spoke, making clear which of the ideas in your essay originated in these sources. Similarly, now that you are writing from written texts, you need to indicate the individual authors whose words and ideas you have included. Citing this information presents you as an honest writer, but even more significantly, it adds great strength to your own writing. For you will be supplementing your own authority with the authority of another, published writer. Or, if you are refuting an author's words, you strengthen your claim by showing that the argument you are making is in response to an ongoing, published conversation.

As we indicated earlier, different disciplines value different kinds of information. And even among those that value the support of written texts, the particular kind of text may vary. For example, your essay may be supported most effectively by quotations from the primary text (the novel, play, or poem you're analyzing), secondary sources (articles or books about the primary text), or statistical evidence from your own research or from others'. Whatever the discipline calls for, there are some common conventions you should know for quoting or paraphrasing from written texts.

1. In a direct quotation writers use someone else's words or sentences as they originally appeared and insert them into their own writing. When you use a direct quotation, be sure to quote *exactly* from the original source, without changing any words or punctuation.

2. When you use part of a direct quotation, your own words need to appropriately and grammatically introduce the quote. Make the others' words fit into the structure of your sentence.

3. Check to be sure you have used both opening and closing quotation marks to indicate the complete quotation for the reader.

4. Whether you use direct quotations that repeat others' words or indirect quotations that paraphrase or summarize them, you must identify the original source either with a parenthetical notation that corresponds to a list of authors and texts on a Works Cited page or with a footnote that corresponds to a notation at the bottom of the

page. Even electronic sources must be cited to include the author's name; the article or document title in quotation marks; the newsletter, journal, or conference title; the number of the pages or paragraphs; the medium of publication as *online*; the computer network name; and the access date.

Whether you use a parenthetical notation or a footnote number depends, in part, on the editorial style conventions of the discipline in which you are writing. Notice that the essays included in Chapter 14 conform to MLA style documentation, using parenthetical citations with a Works Cited page at the end of the text. In addition to the Modern Language Association, several other style formats exist, such as American Psychological Association, Turabian, and Chicago. Your own handbook most likely includes descriptions of each. Find out which one your instructor expects you to use, and then follow its citation guidelines. Though the differences among them may appear slight, to the readers who expect a certain style, they are, indeed, significant.

Works Cited

Belanoff, Pat, Peter Elbow, and Sheryl I. Fontaine. 1991. *Nothing Begins with N: New Investigations of Freewriting*. Carbondale: Southern Illinois Univ. Press.

Berlin, James. 1987. *Rhetoric and Reality: Writing Instruction in American Colleges, 1900–1985*. Carbondale: Southern Illinois Univ. Press.

Berthoff, Anne. 1981. *The Making of Meaning: Metaphors, Models and Maxims for Writing Teachers*. Portsmouth, NH: Boynton/Cook-Heinemann.

Brereton, John. 1995. *The Origins of Composition Studies in the American College, 1875–1925: A Documentary*. Pittsburgh: Univ. of Pittsburgh Press.

Connors, Robert. 1997. *Composition-Rhetoric: Backgrounds, Theory, and Pedagogy*. Pittsburgh: Univ. of Pittsburgh Press.

Cooper, Lane, trans. and ed. 1960. *The Rhetoric of Aristotle*. New York: Prentice-Hall.

Elbow, Peter. 1985. "The Shifting Relationships Between Speech and Writing." *College Composition and Communication* 36: 283–303.

———. 1998. *Writing with Power: Techniques for Mastering the Writing Process*. 2nd ed. New York: Oxford Univ. Press.

———. 1998. *Writing Without Teachers*. 2d ed. New York: Oxford Univ. Press.

Emig, Janet. 1983. *The Web of Meaning*. Portsmouth, NH: Boynton/Cook-Heinemann.

Faigley, Lester. 1986. "Competing Theories of Process: A Critique and a Proposal." *College English* 48 (October): 527–42.

Fox, Tom. 1999. *Defending Access: A Critique of Standards in Higher Education*. Portsmouth, NH: Boynton/Cook-Heinemann.

Gendlin, Eugene. 1982. *Focusing*. New York: Bantam.

Kitzhaber, Alfred. 1990. *Rhetoric in American Colleges, 1850–1900*. Dallas, TX: Southern Methodist Univ. Press.

Kroll, Barry M., and Roberta J. Vann, eds. 1981. *Exploring Speaking-Writing Relationships.* Urbana, IL: National Council of Teachers of English.

Labov, William. 1972. *Language in the Inner City: Studies in Black English Vernacular.* Philadelphia: Univ. of Pennsylvania Press.

Lamott, Anne. 1995. *Bird by Bird: Some Instructions on Writing and Life.* New York: Anchor.

Macrorie, Ken. 1995. *Telling Writing.* Portsmouth, NH: Boynton/Cook-Heinemann.

Moffett, James. 1987. *Teaching the Universe of Discourse.* Portsmouth, NH: Boynton/Cook-Heinemann.

Murray, Donald. 2004. *Write to Learn.* Boston: Heinle.

Nystrand, Martin. 1982. *What Writers Know: The Language, Process, and Structure of Written Discourse.* New York: Academic.

Ong, Walter. 1982. *Orality and Literacy.* New York: Methuen.

Perl, Sondra. 1979. "The Composing Process of Unskilled College Writers." *Research in the Teaching of English* 13:317–36.

———. 2004. *Felt Sense: Writing with the Body.* Portsmouth, NH: Boynton/Cook-Heinemann.

———. ed. 1994. *Landmark Essays on Writing Process.* Davis, CA: Hermagoras.

Rose, Mike. 1985. *When a Writer Can't Write: Studies in Writer's Block and Other Composing Problems.* New York: Guildford.

Scribner, Sylvia, and Michael Cole. 1981. *The Psychology of Literacy.* Cambridge: Harvard Univ. Press.

Smitherman, Geneva. 1977/1986. *Talkin and Testifyin: The Language of Black America.* Detroit: Wayne State Univ. Press.

Smitherman-Donaldson, Geneva. 1987. "Toward a National Public Policy on Language." *College English* 49: 29–36.

Sommers, Nancy. 1980. "Revision Strategies of Student Writers and Experienced Adult Writers." *College Composition and Communication* 31 (December): 378–88.

Swales, John M. 1990. *Genre Analysis: English in Academic and Research Settings.* Cambridge, UK: Cambridge Univ. Press.

Wright, Michael. 2006. Independent Study Project. Department of English, Sacramento, CA: California State University, Sacramento.